To Mom,
   May Christmas find you
Well and among kindred
hearts,
                  Love,
                  Ray & Jean

A Song in Siberia

A Song in Siberia

Anita and Peter Deyneka, Jr.

David C. Cook Publishing Co.

ELGIN, ILLINOIS—WESTON, ONTARIO
LA HABRA, CALIFORNIA

A SONG IN SIBERIA
© 1977 David C. Cook Publishing Co.

Published by David C. Cook Publishing Co., 850 N. Grove Ave., Elgin, IL 60120. Printed in the United States of America.

ISBN 0-89191-065-4

LC 77-70790

And he who sings not with us today
is against
us!

—Vladimir Maiakovskii

CONTENTS

PREFACE

SIBERIA IS the forbidding land of eternal winter and prison camps. It is also the 4,000-mile-wide scenic frontier of the U.S.S.R. where today 40 million people are developing the world's richest natural resources. Located east of the Ural Mountain range, Siberia encompasses more than sixty percent of the Soviet Union.

Barnaul (pronounced bar-na-*ool*), the scene of this book, is one of Siberia's important industrial centers, with a population nearing half a million. It is the capital of the Altai region, located roughly a thousand miles east of the Urals, two thousand miles west of the Pacific, and 125 miles south of Novosibirsk, Siberia's largest and leading city. Barnaul lies on the Ob River, where temperatures range from 100° F. to colder than -60° F.

During its long and tortured history, Siberia has become synonymous with suffering. Most recently, Aleksandr Solzhenitsyn, in his book *The Gulag Archipelago*, has documented the existence of Stalin's sinister chain of prison camps stretched from European Russia across Siberia.

Through its persecuted past and even to the present,

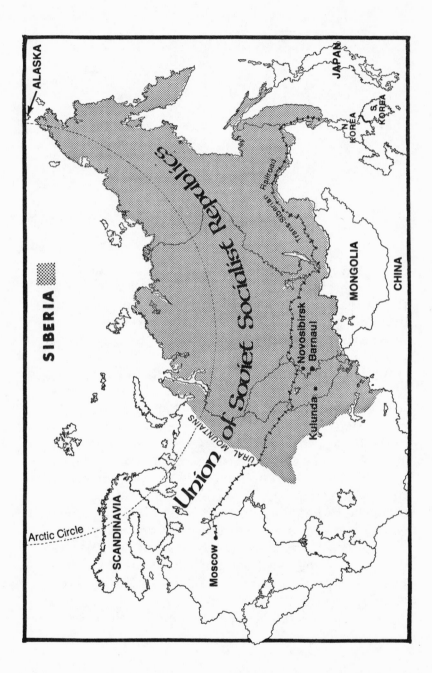

Christian prisoners, exiles, and immigrants have carried their faith to remote Siberia. The blood of the martyrs has become the seed of the church. Siberian churches have not only survived, but today they are vigorous and vibrant.

A part of the story of the church in Siberia is told in this book through the experiences of one congregation.

In 1973 Ivan and Galia M. emigrated from Barnaul to West Germany, where we first met them. Their three-room resettlement apartment bulged with their family of eight children. As we talked, the family settled into a close circle around the table.

Galia spoke softly, reliving life in the Soviet Union, from where the family had come only three months before. Safe in West Germany, scheduled soon to move into a new house, secure and united with relatives, Galia still could not help weeping. She missed Siberia—a land she had grown to love. She still worried about the Christians back home.

Galia groped for her husband's hand as the memories swept over her. "For eleven years the authorities persecuted our church. Some of our members sat in prison. Then in 1972 they started to interrogate our children. The KGB investigator came to school and called them from class. It was so terrible we withdrew them from school," she recalled.

In 1973, 1975, and again in 1976 we spent several days with Russian-German Christians such as Ivan and Galia who had recently been allowed to emigrate from the Soviet Union. Hour after hour we asked them questions we had never been able to discuss freely inside the surveillant society of the U.S.S.R.

11

We were stirred and strengthened as we listened to their story that seemed to us an incredible saga of both suffering and spiritual triumph. We were struck by the similarity of the Russian church to the first-century church in the Book of Acts.

The Christians assured us that their life in Barnaul was not unique—not just an isolated instance. "The same events were happening in churches across the country," they told us, "and they are still happening."

We returned home and transcribed our many hours of conversations with them. We also visited Keston College in England, a research center for the study of religion and communism.

From there and elsewhere we began gathering documents dispatched over a span of several years by the Barnaul church. Since the early sixties, this congregation has sent approximately 300 letters and telegrams to Soviet officials, the United Nations, other churches in the U.S.S.R., and elsewhere. Many of these have reached the West. We also studied documents sent from other churches in Russia recording similar tribulations during this time. Related articles in the Soviet press were traced to compare the official perspective.

This book is the composite of all these perspectives. Primarily, we have tried to let the participants tell their own story. The material has been used with their permission.

As part of the Body of Christ, Christians in Russia long for communication and unity with other members of the Body—including the Church outside of Russia from which they are severed by the Iron Curtain. In their "Appeal to All Christians of the World," the Barnaul Christians wrote, "We believe that our sufferings are your sufferings, for whether one member suffer, all the members suffer with it" (I Corinthians 12: 26).

The Barnaul Christians believe their suffering has been a part of God's plan—a chapter in church history not yet completed:

> Beloved, today we, as children of the covenant and prophets, continue the last pages of the Bible; today we ourselves inscribe and conclude the history of the Church of Christ on earth. We conclude the construction of the mystery hidden from eternity in God, who created all things by Jesus Christ (Ephesians 3: 9).

The Barnaul Christians urge other churches to also record their history:

> As we read the precious verses of the Book of Books, the law and revelation of God to men, we find that already in very ancient times and later in the life of the people of Israel various books and stories, records and letters, were written (II Chronicles 32: 32; Joshua 10: 13; Nehemiah 7: 5). We notice that for this purpose there were special historians and scribes (II Kings 18: 37).
>
> Also, both the New Testament and the Good News of salvation and forgiveness of sins through Jesus Christ were given to the world through simple, modest Galilean residents and fishermen whom God made evangelists and recorders. Their writings until now have served as inexhaustible food for the hearts and minds of millions who have sought and found Christ. Books written over a period of almost two thousand years of the history of the Church of Christ under the inspiration of the Word of God of the Old and New Testaments have constituted the greatest part of the unexplored treasure of human thought. . . .
>
> Our wish before the Lord today is that he will call from our midst and our times such scribes and recorders as in ancient days and in the period of the founding and confirm-

ing of the church when the New Testament was written by blood (Ephesians 4: 12; Romans 16: 22; Luke 1: 1-3). In this way, many people in our day also may read and learn of all the wonderful deeds of our Lord, who yesterday, today, and forever is the same (Hebrews 13: 8).

Thus, dear brothers and sisters, we appeal to those of you who have still not begun to write all the events taking place in your lives and to whom God has revealed the importance of describing his glorious works in your churches. Take your pen and begin to write and describe everything as your life and service passes by.

Part of the story of the church in Barnaul is an account of confrontation between the Christians and their atheistic government. This conflict does not mean that all Russian Christians invariably oppose every aspect of their Soviet state and would instantly emigrate if they had opportunity.

Like the majority of Soviet citizens, most Russian Christians are patriots of Mother Russia. For example, Christian reformer Georgii Vins, now in a Siberian prison, has written a poem entitled "My Love and My Song is Russia."[1] Even the Russian-Germans who emigrated from Barnaul in the 1970s told us they left Russia only as a last resort.

The Barnaul Christians and believers across the U.S.S.R. have tried to work within the structure of their own Soviet legal system. However, in some instances, discrimination against believers is built into Soviet laws. Also, laws are often interpreted capriciously by the authorities.

A 1969 letter to "all Christians of the world" from the Council of Prisoners' Relatives in the Soviet Union states:

We declare to you all that in the revival movement in our

14

land, there is not the slightest resistance to or disobedience of the state. During the last eight years, we have presented our petitions by the thousands in writing and through representative delegations . . . . Our petitions over and over expressly acknowledge the high calling of state authority. In response we receive a persecution that is even stronger and more terrible.

The Baptist church in Barnaul described here is an unregistered church—the kind often referred to as "underground" in the West, although the Russian believers themselves do not use this term. The Barnaul Christians have repeatedly requested permission from government officials to register openly as a recognized church with rights they feel are granted by the Soviet constitution, which guarantees "freedom of religious worship" in Article 124.

Many Baptist, Evangelical Christian, Pentecostal, and Mennonite churches in the U.S.S.R. (approximately five thousand of them) have received permission from the Soviet government to register officially under the All-Union Council of Evangelical Christians-Baptists (AUCECB), organized in 1944.

The Barnaul congregation described here originally belonged to the AUCECB. Through circumstances explained in this book, many of the members joined a reform movement organized in the early sixties when a group of Baptist ministers under the leadership of Aleksei F. Prokofev and Gennadii Kriuchkov, later joined by Georgii Vins, formed the *Initsiativnaia Gruppa,* an action group for the calling of a national Baptist congress. By organizing a congress and electing new leadership, the action group hoped to bring about certain reforms within the AUCECB.

When this failed, the reformers organized their own

15

orgkomitet (governing body). Eventually, they organized a separate union of unregistered churches—the CCECB (Council of Churches of Evangelical Christians-Baptists). The Barnaul congregation described in this book belongs to the CCECB.

In depicting the persecution of the unregistered Barnaul CCECB congregation, we in no way mean to imply that only Christians from unregistered churches live righteously in Soviet society or suffer educational, economic, psychological, and social pressures and in some instances, even imprisonment.* Registered churches are also experiencing surging spiritual vitality, especially in the Ukraine.

The distinction between the two groups is not always clear. Many Russian believers participate in both registered and unregistered congregations in the same city. Some Baptist churches which have not been able to obtain official registration still consider themselves affiliated with the AUCECB. Also, a few congregations previously associated with the CCECB have now been allowed to register independently.

In any case, both registered and unregistered churches face difficulties in an avowedly atheistic Soviet society, although the degree of persecution varies from place to place within the Soviet Union. At certain times in certain places, the Soviet government has made life more difficult for believers. The period in Barnaul from 1961 through 1972 was one such ordeal.

---

*It should be noted that ninety-nine percent of Russian Christians are not in prison. Presently in the Soviet Union there are an estimated 100,000 political prisoners, among whom religious believers (Orthodox, Catholics, Jews, Muslims, and Protestants) are included. It is impossible to estimate how many of these 100,000 are in prison because of their religious convictions. A report received from Russian believers in early 1977 lists 110 prisoners from CCECB congregations.

The severe persecution of the Barnaul church does not make it possible to generalize that all Christians in the Soviet Union are treated identically. The Soviet government has seemed particularly hostile to the Barnaul CCECB congregation, which besides being unregistered has also boldly insisted on civil rights for religious persons. Further, the Barnaul congregation contained many German-Russians—an ethnic group that the Soviets have discriminated against since World War II.

There is one final point the Russian Christians would want us to convey: they are not spiritual supermen. They are ordinary people who become discouraged by the deprivations and tribulations of having to live in a militantly atheistic society. However, they believe that God is King of the universe and that he has not erred in allowing their church to be purged and purified for a more powerful witness. Significantly, Christians in the city of Barnaul have seen the Holy Spirit regenerate many people educated as atheists.

They would say that the secret of spiritual triumph lies in God's supernatural grace, which "is able to keep you from falling, and to present you faultless before the presence of his glory with exceeding joy" (Jude 24).

Whenever last names are used in this book, these are actual names. First names with initials indicate pseudonyms. A similar procedure has been used for names of locations. In some instances it is possible to use actual names of people and places—in fact, the Russian-Germans asked us to do that. In other cases, for protection of the people who remain there, it is not possible.

In this book the terms *Russia, Soviet Union,* and

U.S.S.R. are used interchangeably. Russian words used in the text have been transliterated according to the Library of Congress system.

For providing many of the documents from Christians in the Soviet Union and other information we are grateful to the Reverend Michael Bourdeaux and Keston College, Heathfield Road, Keston, Kent, England BR2 6BA.

For translations of articles from the Soviet press and other information we thank the Reverend Blahoslav S. Hruby and *Religion in Communist-Dominated Areas,* a scholarly publication on the religious situation under communism published by the Research Center for Religion and Human Rights in Closed Societies, Ltd., 475 Riverside Drive, Room 475, New York, NY 10027.

We also wish to thank Dr. Paul D. Steeves, assistant professor of history and director of Russian studies at Stetson University, DeLand, Florida, for checking the manuscript. We appreciate the editorial assistance of Verne Becker in preparing this manuscript.

Mostly we are indebted to the bold believers of Barnaul, who often at great peril preserved their story in the documents and open letters of which this book is a retelling.

1. *Georgi Vins: Testament from Prison* (Elgin, Ill.: David C. Cook, 1975) pp. 256-57.

The Foreign Uncle

YELENA PAVLOVNA CLUTCHED her husband's hand. She wanted to cling to him and cry, *"Opasno*—it is too dangerous! I can't let you go to Moscow, Viktor." But the somber eyes of her two small daughters who stood beside her husband stopped her.

Besides, she sensibly reminded herself, glancing around the Siberian railroad station, *people might be watching. The police could overhear.*

On a bench near Yelena, an old man slept with his gray head propped on a pile of packages wrapped in newsprint. A child, curled in the crook of his mother's strong arm, stared. A *babushka,* her long dark skirt wrapped till it touched her black rubber boots, silently shoved a wet, wadded mop across the stone floor. The people stood, sat, or slumped against the gray walls—waiting. Outside, minutes hurried by on the huge clock on the front of the station.

Families of the other seventeen Christians who had been chosen to travel to Moscow huddled in small groups around the windowless waiting room brightened only by a sign in bold red letters that said, THE THOUGHTS OF LENIN WILL LIVE FOREVER. They had scattered cautiously—careful not to betray their acquaintance. All were struggling not to show the slightest sign of anything amiss as they said good-bye to relatives they might never see again.

Yelena knelt beside Polina, nine, and Liuba, six. The two girls stood bravely by their father, wide-eyed at the prospect of an 1,800-mile, 3-day train trip to Moscow. Yelena fumbled with a loose button on Liuba's blue canvas coat, then straightened the white ribbons in Polina's tight braids. She could not keep from clasping the two children in her arms.

She remembered the day several weeks before when Polina had come home from school trembling, her face streaked with tears. "The investigator called me from class, mama," Polina had stuttered with terror. "He wanted to know where the Christians meet. He asked me if we have a Bible. He wants to know if we listen to the broadcasts. . . ."

But the Americans at the embassy in Moscow . . . Yelena now tried to convince herself. *Surely they will be moved by the harassment of helpless children.*

She thought of her six other children at home. "All of us will pray. You must stay close beside papa," she murmured to her daughters.

. A policeman, the gold stars on his red epaulet reflecting the low railroad station lights, strolled near the family. Yelena stiffened. "Be sure the girls keep their coats buttoned," she told Viktor calmly. "They say it sometimes snows in Moscow even in May."

Snow sprinkled the streets when the twenty believers from the city of Barnaul (bar-na-*ool*), Siberia, stepped off the train at Moscow's Yaroslavskii station on May 9, 1972.

20

The spring wind swirled cold and foreboding.

Following the strategy they had planned and prayed over on the train, the Christians—fourteen adults and six children—broke into three groups. Scouts were selected from each. They strolled casually among the pedestrians sprinkled along the well-swept sidewalks of Tchaikovsky Street, passed the American embassy, and cautiously surveyed the territory beyond the spiked iron fence enclosing the big building. They knew that, legally, Soviet citizens are permitted to enter the embassy. But they also knew that, in reality, entry was forbidden. Ivan Y., an unobtrusive man, was chosen to stand at a distance from the three groups and observe. He would return home to report to the believers in Barnaul in case all the others were arrested.

At two-thirty that afternoon the three groups gathered inconspicuously in a nearby park and prayed together. Then everyone walked back toward the embassy. The American flag beckoned from the front of the building. Formidable Russian policemen sternly guarded the three arched entryways leading from the sidewalk into the embassy courtyard. If only they could dash past the police, if somehow they could gain the few feet from the sidewalk past the iron gate and into the courtyard, the Siberians knew they would be safe inside American territory. Their story would be heard.

At a sign from one of the men, the Christians suddenly surged toward the arch. Viktor grasped Polina and Liuba by the hand. "I shut my eyes and shoved through the archway," Viktor recalls. "The Russian policeman grabbed my friend Vasilii, who was in front of me, his child in his arms, and knocked him to his knees. But he clung to the child and struggled through the entrance.

"At that moment someone shoved Polina. She was

21

thrown toward the iron fence. Miraculously, she was not hurt, and to this day I think an angel put his hand between her head and the post.

"As the *militsiia* began to beat us, we did not strike back, but we started to shout, 'They're killing us, they're killing us!' Some of the Americans came running from the embassy door to see what was happening. During the confusion we kept trying to push through the archway.

"I was knocked down and my shoe torn off. One of the *militsiia* picked it up and began to smash me over the head with it.

"He beat me until I collapsed. In the meantime, one of the women managed to grab my daughters and yank them inside the archway.

"Four of us didn't make it in. The *militsiia* and KGB plainclothesmen who had swiftly arrived on the scene dragged three of us men and a seven-year-old boy, Pavlik, away from the sidewalk and drove us to a police station in a 'Black Maria,' the van for transporting prisoners."

On the way to the station, the prisoners were bombarded with questions. "Who are you? Why did you do it? Why did you disgrace our country?

"And only two weeks before the American president Nixon arrives in Moscow!" one of the *militsiia* sputtered, his face and gray uniform smudged from the scuffle.

When the questioners finally paused, Viktor and the other Christians tried to explain. They pulled photos and documents from their pockets—copies of unanswered letters and telegrams they had repeatedly sent to government officials in Moscow, pleading that persecutions against Christians in Siberia be stopped.

A KGB plainclothesman snatched the folded paper from Viktor's hands. "This is the end of you!" he snapped. "You'll never see daylight again!"

With police linked tightly like a chain around them, the Christians were escorted from the "Black Maria" into the police station. Inside was an uproar. Viktor overheard one policeman inform another, "There are only nineteen of them, but maybe they're part of a larger uprising."

A second man turned to Viktor and demanded, "Where are the rest of your group—where are they hiding?"

Viktor said nothing.

Quickly the officers prepared protocols—papers describing the circumstances of arrest—and demanded that the three men sign them. But the Christians, who suspected from experience that the Soviet police might add charges after the paper had been signed, refused.

Then the police started to threaten. "We know all about you. We have called the authorities in Barnaul. We know how you hold illegal church meetings. You are agitating against Soviet society. You are not fit to eat Soviet bread!"

Pavlik, the seven-year-old, clung to Viktor. His father, mother, younger brother, and two sisters were inside the U.S. embassy building. "Whose boy is this?" said the interrogator, glaring at Pavlik.

Pavlik huddled closer to Viktor. "Please, uncle, tell them I belong to you," he whispered.

Viktor held Pavlik close. "Of course you belong to me, and we belong to Jesus. Jesus will look after your mama and papa and all of us," Viktor comforted the child.

By this time, it was almost midnight. The Christians had eaten nothing since noon. Viktor found a melted piece of chocolate wrapped in red foil inside his pocket and handed it to Pavlik.

After midnight the police finally tired of the interrogation. They shoved the three men and Pavlik into a cell usually reserved for drunks to sleep off their inebriation. A policeman was assigned to guard each of the four Christians as they slept.

But the guards—startled at the sight of three men and a child being thrust into a cell for drunks—were curious. "There must be another reason. It can't be just because you are *veruiushchie*" (believers), a young guard said.

"I never met a Christian before," another guard with bewildered blue eyes mumbled. "I understand you Christians pray. How do you go about this?"

"Well, we will show you," Viktor smiled. To the astonishment of the guards, the four Christians dropped to their knees on the cement floor by the prison bunks. They prayed for the guards and the authorities who had put them in prison. They asked God to comfort their families waiting anxiously back in Barnaul. And they prayed for the fifteen brothers and sisters who they hoped were safe inside the American embassy.

The guards stared. They agreed among themselves that they had never seen anything like it.

The next morning two of the police bought some sausage, bread, and milk for their prisoners with money the Christians provided. "Little Pavlik mustn't go hungry," one of the guards said kindly as he passed the food through the bars.

That morning the interrogations resumed. KGB officials separated the three men and questioned them severely.

"Do you realize that the whole world will know about this episode?" Viktor's interrogator raged. "Your children are inside the American embassy."

He struggled to speak calmly. "You can help straighten out this whole matter," he said. "I'll give you a telephone. You call your friends in the embassy. Tell them to come out. They must tell the Americans it was all a mistake!" He was nearly pleading now.

"But it was not a mistake," Viktor corrected quietly, hoping that perhaps one official might listen at last. Viktor reminded the KGB officer about the documents that had been stripped from him the night before—the list of grievances that made life so intolerable for believers in Barnaul. "Such persecution of honest citizens is a disgrace to our country. Our Soviet laws are supposed to protect against such injustices."

The official was still listening, so Viktor boldly went on. "Even Lenin said that everyone must be perfectly free to belong to whatever religion he pleases and also be free to preach his religion and change his religion.

"And Article 124 of the constitution says that the church in the U.S.S.R. is separated from the state and the school from the church," Viktor persisted.

"I am sure you know, comrade, that the Soviet Union subscribes to the United Nations Declaration of Human Rights. . . ."

But before Viktor could cite more legal support, the KGB officer interrupted. "*Konechno*—of course, Soviet laws strictly uphold the rights of believers. So how is it you dare to allege that they don't? You are slandering Soviet reality," the officer insisted illogically.

Viktor answered wearily with a request. "Please release us and we will join our brothers and sisters at the American embassy. Maybe the Americans will understand. Maybe if the Americans plead our case, our own government leaders will listen."

The answer was no.

Meanwhile, the fifteen who had gotten safely inside the embassy were presenting their case. But however much the Americans might have sympathized, they hesitated to intercede with Soviet officials. They did, however, ask the Russian government not to retaliate against the believers.

"Of course they won't be punished," the Russian official had assured the American attache. "It is not a crime to enter your embassy. The citizens will be sent straight home to their own city—Barnaul."

When the time came the next day for the transfer, the fifteen Siberians implored the Americans to accompany them—"at least as far as the bus."

"But the authorities have promised to take you by bus to the train station," the Americans, who had their own doubts, replied. "There you will meet your four friends and return home. The police have promised not to harm you." Reluctantly, the fifteen filed through the embassy entrance they had entered with such hope the day before.

"We were grabbed like flour sacks and thrown aboard a bus," one woman recounts. "They hurled me against the bus floor." Some of the children clung to the windows crying to passersby, "Please help us! We don't want to go!" Most pedestrians averted their faces and detoured fearfully away from the commotion. Others chided, "They must be hooligans, or the authorities wouldn't treat them like that!" Some stopped and spoke sympathetically, but no one tried to intervene.

Then, as the Christians had suspected, they were driven not to the train but to the police station.

The police herded the fifteen new arrivals into a room next to the four who had already spent one night in prison. Pavlik heard their voices. "Papa! Mama!" he called to his parents through the partition. In a few moments the police opened the doors between the two rooms.

"You can't imagine the reunion we had in prison," Viktor remembers. "With tears of joy we embraced each other and started to sing, pray, and thank God. Polina and Liuba rushed into my arms."

"Papa, we were sleeping on the floor under a table in the embassy!" six-year-old Liuba said. "But I couldn't sleep all night," Polina added soberly. "We prayed all night that we would be together again."

Nearly twenty policemen stood in the crowded room. Most gaped. Tears crept down the ruddy cheeks of one policeman and Viktor heard him mutter, "What kind of business is it to arrest people like this?"

Viktor had saved food from the supply the guard had brought that morning. The Christians divided the food—urging each other to take the larger portion. After eating, they sang, prayed, and praised God again.

After long talks among themselves, one of the chief KGB officials glumly addressed the Christians, "Will you return home peacefully to Barnaul?"

"If you return the money you took from us," Viktor demanded. Not knowing if they would ever be allowed to return home, the Christians had purchased only one-way tickets.

Within hours after the incident at the American embassy, the Christians in Barnaul knew their brothers were in the capricious hands of the Moscow police. Using code words, Ivan Y., the observer, had telephoned the news to them.

27

The local *militsiia* also got the word promptly. Plain-clothes police soon appeared at the home of every family whose relatives had traveled to Moscow.

"Where's your husband?" a KGB officer questioned Viktor's wife Yelena.

"I'm sure you know better than I do," Yelena answered tersely.

"Do you know what bitter consequences your husband's thoughtless trip to Moscow could have for your whole family?" the KGB asked another wife. "Do you really think your husband did the right thing?"

"I wish I could have accompanied him to Moscow," the woman replied firmly.

"You see how dusty my shoes are?" another policeman said when he called at one of the Christians' homes. "All day I've been walking the streets trying to solve this problem—I'm worried about what will happen to your husband, and worried about what will become of you here alone with your children."

"Were you worried about my welfare when you dragged me out of the church by my hair?" the wife retorted. She turned sadly to the policeman. "It is because our own motherland didn't care about our suffering that we had to turn to a foreign uncle. We pray he will have mercy on us."

But the foreign uncle had been able to provide little practical assistance. The Americans had expressed sympathy toward the plea to help publicize the Barnaul persecution. But they were also realistic about the practicalities of their diplomatic position—particularly with Richard Nixon's visit only a few days away.

Reunited in prison, the believers still believed that their decision to enter the American embassy had been part of God's will. Nevertheless, some troubling uncertainties loomed ahead. Would the government actually allow them to return home? Would the publicity of their trip persuade the government to stop persecuting believers in Barnaul and other Christian congregations across the U.S.S.R.?

Unsure of their fate, the nineteen boarded the train which the authorities promised would take them home to their families.

The full meaning of the dramatic 1972 appeal to the American embassy becomes apparent only when placed against the background of the Christians' experience in Barnaul. It is a long story, going back to precommunist times. The following chapters are an attempt to trace that experience, particularly the twelve-year period beginning in 1961, when the spotlight of Soviet pressure against the evangelical faith seemed especially focused on Barnaul.

1

Beginnings

IN 1917, WHEN THE BOLSHEVIK REVOLUTION crushed the already crumbling autocracy of Tsar Nicholas II, Reinhold G. was a teenager—old enough to remember both the Revolution and Russia's struggle against Germany in World War I.

Reinhold was himself a German—a German-Russian. His ancestors had immigrated to Russia in the late 1700s under the reign of Empress Catherine the Great and settled on the fertile farmlands of the Ukraine. Reinhold's parents, like many of the German-Russians in the Ukraine, were "Stundists"—godly Germans who faithfully gathered for Bible study hours *("stunden")*.

Even before the Revolution, life had not been easy for evangelical Christians. The Russian Orthodox Church had strongly opposed the Stundists as well as Baptists in the Ukraine and Caucasus and other evangelical Christians in aristocratic St. Petersburg.

For a few years after the Bolshevik Revolution, life was surprisingly better for evangelicals. Even though restrictions (such as denying the right of juridical personage) were placed on all religious associations, Lenin's new communist government concentrated its attack against the recalcitrant Russian Orthodox Church in its campaign to root out religion. Evangelicals experienced an unprecedented but short-lived freedom. It is estimated that evangelicals numbered approximately a hundred thousand before the Revolution. Under the first ten years of Soviet rule, they grew to about two million adherents.

Reinhold was married and had one child by the time Josef Stalin climbed to power in 1928. In April, 1929, Stalin codified all previous laws on religion into a "Law on Religious Associations" containing sixty-eight articles. Stalin's new laws reinforced a 1922 law which had already stipulated that only churches which registered with the state were allowed to function. However, now the state agency could arbitrarily grant or deny registration and also could control the appointment of church leaders.

To make it consistent with Stalin's new codes, the paragraph in the 1918 constitution which had guaranteed freedom of religion was altered in 1929. The 1918 constitution had said, "In order to guarantee complete freedom of conscience for the workers, the church is separated from the state and the school from the church. The right to religious and antireligious propaganda is recognized for all citizens." The new 1929 code canceled the right to "religious propaganda" and allowed only "freedom of religious worship."

In reality, Stalin's new laws on religion put the Soviet government in a position to control the churches of Russia.

By the 1930s Stalin was deporting Soviet citizens for various reasons to Siberian labor camps and prisons. The Georgian dictator had set in motion the terror that would eventually mean death to at least twenty million.

Reinhold's father, a leader among the Stundists, was one of those exiled to Siberia. Like thousands of other Christians, he died a martyr's death in a labor camp.

But Christians like Reinhold's father viewed their exile as a missionary opportunity. Through footsteps of blood, many churches sprang up across Siberia. One of those churches was in the 200-year-old city of Barnaul where a small cluster of Christians started to meet.

On June 22, 1941, Hitler's army attacked an unprepared Russia. Stalin feared that German-Russians such as Reinhold's family might welcome the Nazi armies as liberators from the terrors of Soviet tyranny. Even though hundreds of German-Russian soldiers were fighting heroically against the Nazi aggressors, Stalin placed citizens of German heritage under a "special settlement" status. They could move about freely only in the area to which they had been assigned, and were penalized if they left that area without authorization. German-Russians needed special permits to buy food and had to report regularly to the police.

Purportedly to prevent collaboration with the Nazis, Stalin resettled hundreds of thousands of Germans in various sections of the Urals and Siberia. He packed the refugees into cattle cars for the arduous train trip east and housed them in crude barracks when they finally reached their destinations. Reinhold, his wife, and their six children were shipped to Barnaul—an industrial city in the Altai Territory of Central Siberia. Situated near Mongolia on the left bank of the large, north-flowing Ob River, it had a population of about 150,000 at that time.

In Barnaul, Reinhold soon met other Christians who were gathering faithfully to worship God. World War II, which threatened to devastate Russia, brought some relief to churches like the group of believers who met in a home in Barnaul. Because Stalin needed to unite Russia's people against the German invaders, he abruptly granted concessions to Orthodox and Protestant churches—whose congregations, ironically, included many German-Russians. These concessions, however, constituted a secret concordat and were only a matter of policy, not public law.

In 1944, the All-Union Council of Evangelical Christians-Baptists (AUCECB), an alliance uniting most evangelical Protestant groups in the Soviet Union into one official denomination, was formed under Soviet government supervision. Some churches previously closed at Stalin's orders were allowed to reopen. From 1944 through 1948 many new congregations were allowed to "register" under the AUCECB—now the gateway to legal legitimacy. One of those was the Barnaul group.

Reinhold recalls that in 1944 "there were about ten of us Christians who gathered in a home. Then we bought a frame house at 67 Radishchevskaia Street, and this was the first Baptist* church building in Barnaul" (see photo section).

"At that time my wife, Yekaterina, and I lived on a *kolkhoz* (collective farm) outside the city." Although Reinhold and his family had come from warmer climates, Siberia soon became home. "We grew accustomed to Barnaul and liked it," Reinhold says simply. "Every Sunday we walked ten kilometers each way to our church—morning and evening."

Stalin died in 1953, and the iron grip of the dictator was broken. After twenty-four years of rule, some Soviet

*Since 1944, almost all evangelical Protestants in the U.S.S.R. have been commonly known as Baptists.

citizens thought the country would not survive without him. Others, such as Reinhold, wondered if freedoms promised in Lenin's Bolshevik Revolution would finally begin to materialize. When Khrushchev denounced Stalin at the 20th Communist Party Congress in February, 1956, hopes soared.

In the late 1950s Khrushchev chose the fertile Altai Territory—the region of which Barnaul is the capital—as a center for his virgin lands project designed to develop Siberian agricultural potential. Pioneers from European Russia, drawn by the challenge of the East, settled among the Germans, Latvians, Estonians, and others whom Stalin had already sent to Barnaul. Some of the new settlers became Christians and joined the church.

By 1958, there were over five hundred members in the Barnaul Baptist Church. Parents who had been terrified of severe Soviet legislation against Christian education during the first half of Stalin's reign now brought their children to church. There were about seventy teenage believers among the Barnaul Christians.

But in the early sixties Khrushchev's government launched a new offensive against religion. Confident of the success of his antireligious campaign, Khrushchev once bragged that he would exhibit the last Christian in the U.S.S.R. on television by 1965.

From 1959 to 1964 an estimated ten thousand Orthodox and Baptist churches were closed. At the same time, Khrushchev and the Communist Party intensified atheistic indoctrination in Soviet schools. The output of atheistic literature was increased. At the 22nd Communist Party Congress in 1961, Khrushchev said:

Communist education presupposes emancipation from religious prejudices and superstitions, which hinder Soviet people from fully developing their creative powers. A well-thought-out and well-proportioned system of scientific atheistic propaganda is necessary to embrace all strata of society and to prevent the spread of religious attitudes, especially among children and juveniles.[1]

In 1964, Leonid F. Ilichev, the secretary of the Central Committee of the Communist Party, asserted:

We cannot remain indifferent to the fate of children whom fanatical religious parents are virtually raping spiritually. We cannot permit blind and ignorant parents to raise children like themselves and thus deform them.[2]

In Barnaul, the antireligious campaign had resumed in 1958. It was then that the Barnaul *upolnomochennyi*, the local government representative from the Council for Affairs of Religious Cults* in Moscow, started to keep closer watch on the church at 67 Radishchevskaia Street. Reinhold remembers the day he insisted, "Young people should not be so involved in church activities. If they must recite poems, they should be the kind that will not attract nonbelievers."

Later the *upolnomochennyi* learned that one of the Christians had taken a photo of the Barnaul youth group (see photo section). He demanded the photo and a list of the names of the young people pictured. "Who among the adults is your youth leader?" he wanted to know.

"We take turns," the Christians replied.

In 1960 the Soviet government pressured the governing body of the AUCECB in Moscow to issue a pastoral

---

*In 1966 the Council for Affairs of Religious Cults and the Council for Russian Orthodox Church Affairs, which had been organized in 1943-44 to provide government supervision of religious activities, were merged into the Council for Religious Affairs.

Letter of Instructions to Baptist presbyters or leaders throughout the nation. The letter was accompanied by the stringent New AUCECB Statutes.

The New Statutes diminished autonomy of local churches and gave more authority to the central body. The statutes further declared that the AUCECB would recognize only congregations which had been legally registered by the Soviet government. A large percentage—possibly as high as two-thirds of all Russian Baptist congregations—had never been able to obtain legal registration from the government. Consequently, the New Statutes effectively cut off unregistered congregations from the national brotherhood of the AUCECB and invited schism.

Among other constricting clauses, the Letter of Instructions to pastors prohibited "unhealthy missionary manifestations." Emphasis on evangelistic preaching was condemned. The baptisms of young people between the ages of eighteen and thirty were to be kept to a minimum. Children were not to attend religious services, and young people under eighteen could not be baptized.

When Reinhold and the other Christians in Barnaul read the New Statutes and heard about the Letter of Instructions, they were aghast. Even though they realized their leaders in Moscow had probably issued the letter at swordpoint, they felt betrayed.

Many believers in Barnaul and in other regions of the Soviet Union felt that obeying these instructions would ruin their churches. Some Baptists tried desperately to call the AUCECB to reformation. They urged the AUCECB to stand boldly against government edicts. Some believers decided either to separate from registered churches of the AUCECB where they found government control intolerable, or in the future not to apply for registration under the AUCECB.

In Barnaul one evening in 1960, the local minister of cults arrived at the church board meeting. Reinhold recalls, "The *upolnomochennyi* insisted that a new man, Yakov Fedorovich Sablin, be installed as chief pastor or presbyter."

The Barnaul believers protested. As accustomed as they were to government surveillance, they insisted that internal affairs of the church must be sacred matter for the local congregation to resolve. Each church should elect its own presbyters, not the central AUCECB or the Soviet government. Furthermore, the Christians had serious doubts about the character of Yakov Sablin. Believers in another town had accused him of drunkenness and immorality.

However, the local communist officials were insistent. "If you don't accept Yakov Fedorovich Sablin as your new presbyter, we'll completely close your church," they threatened.

The believers distrusted Sablin and resented the government's interference. Nevertheless, they agreed they must try to keep their church open. Sadly, they listened to Sablin's sermons urging Christians to be less firm in their faith. One day Sablin announced to his congregation, "I am a communist plus God." The Barnaul believers prayed that the new preacher would either be converted or leave. But Sablin stayed.

Mostly by threats, the minister of cults established a council of twenty leading members *(dvadtsatka)* from the church to carry out his orders. Then he ordered the council to prepare to ordain Sablin. Church members like Reinhold, who objected, were swiftly excommunicated.

At the end of a service, Sablin would simply read a list

of members whom he and local communist authorities had decided to excommunicate that week. There was no appeal, no referral for general vote of the church membership. The government's orders, carried out through the minister of cults, Sablin, and the *dvadtsatka,* were irrevocable.

Finally, several of the church members could endure the heavy-handed interference no longer. At a members' meeting they excommunicated Sablin.

In January, 1961, Comrade A. N. Gorbatenko, vice-president of the Railroad Regional Executive Committee (a municipal/police district in Barnaul), arrived with the *militsiia* and hung locks with seals on the doors of the prayer house at 67 Radishchevskaia Street. The act meant much more than the loss of a place to meet. It signaled the loss of official sanction. As far as the Soviet government was concerned, the Barnaul Baptist Church no longer existed.

1. *Pravda,* October 18, 1962.
2. Leonid F. Ilichev, "Formirovanie Nauchnogo Mirovozreniia i Ateisticheskoe Vospitanie" ("The Formation of a Scientific World Outlook and Atheistic Education.") *Kommunist,* No. 1, 1964, p. 30.

2

From House to House

The sea of life is raging
Round my boat relentlessly.
Desperate and despairing,
I cry, my only Hope, to thee.

Regard with your compassion
My long struggle to be free.
Battered by exhaustion,
I beg mercy, God, from thee.

—Ivan Prokhanoff

Thrust out of their registered church building in 1961,
the congregation of Baptists in Barnaul began to meet in
homes. Battered by a storm of opposition from the Soviet
government, they tried to cling together as a church.

All across Russia, similar persecutions were ravaging
other churches. For example, in Vladivostok, a Siberian
city far to the east, Soviet authorities had torn down the
registered church. The believers there continued to meet
in a nearby house that was little more than a hovel. They
hammered a roof onto the dilapidated building and,
despite much difficulty, gathered there year around.

Meanwhile, in Barnaul, the *upolnomochennyi* and Comrade Gorbatenko began insisting that it was illegal for believers to meet anywhere—unless they registered according to the regulations of Stalin's 1929 law. They further demanded that the Christians must obey the infamous New AUCECB Statutes and Letter of Instructions.

The believers did eventually apply three times for registration after the government locked them out of their church on Radishchevskaia Street. They scrupulously submitted the required information such as the number of members in the congregation, the signatures of the *dvadtsatka,* the names of committee members, and their places of employment.

Their petitions were fruitless. One of the Christians comments, "The law states that authorities are legally required to say yes or no within a month of receiving a registration application. But as far as we know, our registration applications are still lying in a government office."

"If you want to register," communist officials insisted, "you must adhere to the new regulations. You must curtail evangelistic activities and you must not bring your children to church."

Thus they were caught between their desire for legal recognition and for continued spiritual life. The government would not allow both.

So the Baptists continued meeting in homes without government sanction. They were not the first group to do so. Pentecostals, Seventh-Day Adventists, Lutherans, Mennonites, some Russian Orthodox, and other groups who had been refused registration (or found it impossible to meet under the restrictions of registration) were also gathering in homes by 1961.

43

When they were expelled from their church, the Baptists switched from home to home to hold their services. Later they settled into one home as their meeting place, concluding that "the unity gave us a stronger witness."

Squeezing 150 to 200 people into one or even a few homes was not a simple matter, especially in Russia, where most people live in two- or three-room apartments. Believers did not regularly use apartments for church services, but when a family first moved into an apartment it was possible to hold housewarmings. Christians packed a few small rooms, sang, prayed, and preached. When police complained that Christians were conducting a Gospel meeting, they replied, "No—a housewarming!"

A few members of the now unregistered congregation owned small homes, and these provided the best meeting places. Leonid R., who lived in a log house that had belonged to his parents and grandparents, often opened his home to the other believers. "The day before the meeting, my wife and children helped me move our furniture into the garden. Our house was so small that we decided to remove the wall between two of the rooms to make more space for the meeting."

Wherever they met, the believers discreetly tried not to disturb the neighborhood. They reminded their children not to linger outside the door. But despite their caution, their meetings in the closely-watched Soviet society did not go unnoticed. The police insisted that they were guilty of "disturbing the peace and also meeting secretly." These accusations were used as a pretext for prosecution, even though Article 143 of the penal code of the RSFSR (Russian Soviet Federated Socialist Republic) states it is "an offense to hinder the celebration of religious rites which do not disturb the public."

Avram L., a believer from Barnaul, laughs ruefully when he recalls the accusation of secrecy. "No matter how hard we tried to meet quietly and peacefully, our meetings could not be called secret or underground. In our country any gathering attracts attention, and the neighbors and police soon knew we were a church. Besides, the KGB often published articles attacking us in the newspaper. Even though there were only 150 to 200 of us Christians meeting, I think the whole city of Barnaul with its 350,000 people knew about our church!

"Sometimes when we walked to the home where our church was held, children from the neighborhood hurled stones at us and hollered, 'Baptists!' Other neighbors came out to see what was causing the commotion. No, our meeting was not a secret—to the authorities or to our neighbors."

Hoping for evidence to halt the house meetings, KGB representatives visited people in nearby neighborhoods to collect damaging evidence against the Christians. "Are those religious fanatics bothering, embarrassing, or harming you in any way?" they asked hopefully. Bribed by a bottle of vodka, some neighbors were willing to invent complaints against the Christians.

But not all non-Christian neighbors showed hostility. Many expressed curiosity and interest. The police feared that these people would be attracted to the joyful meetings. One of the Barnaul pastors explains, "When we met in a house, the police would not permit us to open any windows facing the street—only windows facing unoccupied courtyards."

Some neighbors stoutly defended the Christians and even admitted attending the meetings. "Their singing cheers our whole neighborhood," one woman who was not a believer told the police.

The *upolnomochennyi* himself sometimes came to the Christian meetings to gather evidence against the believers. He meticulously recorded hymn titles, Scripture references, sermon topics, and even jotted down the words the Christians used when praying for him.

On one occasion he stood up during the meeting and abruptly announced, "I demand an immediate discussion with the leaders of the church. You have preached—now I will preach to you!"

The believers were not interested in a diatribe against Christianity. "Why do you meddle in our affairs?" they asked. "Our laws say the church and state are separate. We do not interfere with matters of state."

On another occasion when a discussion was demanded during a service, the pastor took a vote. "Are you willing to remain for a discussion with the *upolnomochennyi?*" he asked. The weary Christians shouted in unison, "No!"

As months of cross-examinations by the KGB officials wore on, some Christians refused to answer summonses for questionings. "Why should we come?" they boldly told the police. "We know what you believe and you know what we believe. You attend our meetings and hear us preach. We won't convince you and you won't convince us. We don't have time to quarrel about these matters. We know you are collecting material and want to arrest us. We will not willingly be interrogated."

When the Christians resisted, determined KGB officials ordered reinforcements. Either the intransigent Christians would stop their meetings, or register—under government surveillance.

On October 19, 1963, at a harvest festival held in Y. D. Mantai's home, KGB agents, fire department employees, and press and television editors invaded the meeting. Comrade Konosov, the president of the October Regional Executive Committee (a local jurisdiction), led the delegation that also included police and civil guards.

Most often the authorities simply sent *druzhinniki* to disrupt the Christian meetings. The *druzhinniki,* ostensibly a volunteer auxiliary police detachment, gave the appearance of legality—a collective of Soviet citizens rising righteously to protest the activities of Christians. And what happened if the *druzhinniki* went to excess in their anger? The Soviet officials who had given them the orders in the first place could shrug its shoulders and say, "The will of the people must be obeyed."

Uninvited *druzhinniki* came to the Christian meetings with portable microphones, loudspeaking systems, and noisemakers. As soon as the singing started, the noise began. Sometimes they shouted, "Christians are the enemies of the people!" Often the *druzhinniki* brought hand-turned sirens used for fire signals and cranked them while the choir sang. The believers simply sang louder and louder—sometimes until the arms of the *druzhinniki* drooped from winding the noisemakers.

At first the *druzhinniki* silenced their disruptions when the Christians stood or knelt to pray. Grateful, the congregation extended their prayers while the *druzhinniki* squirmed. But when the prayers continued for more than an hour, the *druzhinniki* began to shout, "Comrades, stop this foolishness. Why are you allowing yourselves to be deceived by religion?"

Rapidly, the *druzhinniki* and *militsiia* discovered that discussions and disruptions did not dissuade the believers. So they began to levy fines against Christians who used their homes for meetings. The first time, the fine was usually fifty rubles—about half a month's salary. Sometimes fines went as high as one hundred rubles or more.

Often the determined Christians paused just long enough to take an offering, pay the fine, and continue their meeting. If the owner and the other Christians did not have enough money, the police subtracted the fine from the owner's future salary.

Vladimir K., a poor pensioner, was fined by the Barnaul authorities for using his simple frame house as a church. Vladimir, who received a pension of only 13 rubles a month, had no cash. But he did have a yard full of chickens.

When he could not pay, the *militsiia* leader shouted, "If that is the case, comrade, we will confiscate your chickens to pay your fine!"

"But they are not easy to catch," Vladimir smiled faintly.

The Christians continued their meeting while the *militsiia* stomped out the door swearing at the indignity of their assignment. While the congregation sang, the police chased chickens in the courtyard until they had scooped a gunnysackful.

Unfortunately, the police did more than threaten and fine the Christians.

For example, the police often stood at the front of the church and harassed the choir and preachers. To counter this, the congregation resolved to arrive early for their meetings. They stood in a tight circle and formed a solid wall that they hoped would prevent the police from disturbing their worship.

"But the police literally walked over us," Sofia T. remembers. Her arm had been twisted and bruised by a policeman when he rudely shoved her to the floor as he tore his way through a meeting.

Tougher *druzhinniki* were sent to replace the ones who had been silent during prayer. Some Komsomol (Young Communist League) teenagers, braced by all the free alcohol they could drink, cut their way violently through the crowd of Christians. The *Komsomoltsy* brutalized believers, who they had been told were dangerous fanatics threatening communist society. When the Christians tried to take photos of the terror that had come to their meetings, the police and *druzhinniki* ripped the cameras from their hands.

The police not only searched homes where meetings were held—they even invaded the homes of believers who only attended the meetings. The *druzhinniki,* their red arm bands tied tightly around their left arms, came with search warrants authorizing them to look for anti-Soviet literature. Any Bibles, hymnbooks, or other Christian literature that they discovered were confiscated.

Sometimes the police installed bugging devices in the Christian homes they searched. Lidiia and Ivan M., a Christian couple, lived on the east side of Barnaul. In the spring of 1962 their house was searched. After the police were safely distant from the house, Lidiia remarked with relief to her husband, "I'm so thankful they didn't find the Bible we hid in the baby's crib."

The next day the police returned, marched straight to the baby's crib, and seized the Bible. Lidiia and Ivan later found a small microphone hidden behind the cupboard in their kitchen.

The Barnal believers were a minority in their city. In 1962, they were also among a minority of Russian Protestants outside AUCECB—related churches.

But by 1962, the Soviet government was sincerely worried by the bold activities of believers in Barnaul and elsewhere who had become separated from the

AUCECB and even claimed to represent the evangelical Christians and Baptists in Russia. The Soviet government was not accustomed to Christians bravely demanding their constitutional rights.

Up to 1960, unregistered congregations across Russia had no central organization and little contact with each other. Now, intensified government interference was molding Christians across Russia into a national reform movement. Pleading for revival and purification of AUCECB churches, fiery Christian leaders such as Aleksei F. Prokofev, Gennadii K. Kriuchkov, and Georgii P. Vins came to the forefront of the reform movement and formed an *Initsiativnaia Gruppa* ("action group"). Many Christians from Barnaul actively supported the *Initsiativniki.*

Having failed to stop the house meetings of the *Initsiativniki,* the local government decided to try other tactics. In a startling move, they reopened the registered Baptist church. Almost two years after it had been closed, the registered prayer house at 67 Radishchevskaia Street was reopened on Christmas Eve, 1962, by the authorities in the presence of the police, civil guards, and a commissioner on religious cults of the district executive committee. Soviet authorities recalled D. I. Babich, who had earlier served as Barnaul presbyter, from Alma-Ata to replace Yakov Sablin. (Sablin stayed on in a small house near the church, but turned against the believers. He later became active in Bezbozhnik, an anti-God organization, and wrote a book denouncing Christians.)

The government invited the Barnaul believers to return to their church building—but under the government's conditions. Most of the congregation tried to return. However, *druzhinniki* halted believers at the door who insisted on bringing their children or who would not bow to other government restrictions.

Thus, many believers determined to continue their house meetings despite difficulties they feared would follow. They had tried and were trying to obey the laws of their country. Now they felt they must obey the laws of God above all else.

Timofei R., an elderly lay preacher whose wrinkled face records the suffering of those years, explains, "When we had problems and persecutions, we knew it was because the officials of the kingdom of earth could not see the Kingdom of God. They could not understand that we believers live in two worlds!"

3

The Body Alive

AS MORE AND MORE unregistered churches sprang up across the country in the 1960s, officials frantically tried to discourage any religious curiosity among Soviet citizens. Crude propaganda articles attacking believers and their "barbarian" practices poured from government presses. One newspaper article entitled "Once Upon a Time There Was a Little Girl," described how a grandmother had "crippled" the life of her eight-year-old granddaughter Tania by leading her into the path of religion.

Graphically, the article depicted the Baptist meeting where Tania was taken by her grandmother:

People sang, went through strange motions, and entered into ecstasy that was meaningless and strange to the little girl. The people, including her own grandmother puzzled the little girl. Their actions drove her into a state of dread. It was not the usual autumn chill but the icy atmosphere of fear that penetrated little Tania's heart. Weeks and months went by. Almost every Sunday the Baptist heresy was dinned into the girl's mind.

According to this article, Tania suffered so much from attending Baptist meetings that she now had a "serious nervous affliction, weakened cardiac activity, and incipient rheumocarditis."[1]

In contrast to Soviet propaganda descriptions, the actual order of worship at Baptist meetings in Barnaul in the 1960s—and in other congregations, registered and unregistered, across Russia—was strikingly different.

Believers came quietly and usually early to worship services. As soon as two or three gathered, they started to sing, finding a spiritual strength in unity. If someone had a piece of Christian literature from the West, he stood and read aloud to the others. Another Christian fortunate enough to own a Bible or a portion of Scripture shared his treasure.

Then singing rose spontaneously again—almost always from memory—since few people other than the choir director owned a hymn book. This preservice, warm and worshipful, continued for as long as an hour before the scheduled service actually began.

"During our services we felt it was important for everyone to have an opportunity to use his spiritual gifts," one of the Barnaul lay pastors who now lives in Germany explains. "We were one body, and each of the believers wanted to participate in worship. This way we shared one another's burdens and also shared in the suffering of Christ."

In Barnaul, eight to twelve men took turns preaching. None of the regular preachers were university graduates. Some had tried to enter universities but were rejected when it was discovered they were Christians.

None of the men had any formal theological training, since there are no Protestant Bible schools or seminaries in the Soviet Union.*

The preachers chose strictly biblical sermon texts. Illustrations were largely selected from the Bible, seldom from modern life. Preachers took constant care that nothing in their sermons could be construed as anti-Soviet or political by government officials and informers who regularly came to monitor the service.

The choir always sang several times during the service. "To us the songs were more than songs—they were sermons," one expatriate choir member explains. "They had come from the lives and sufferings of our brothers and sisters across our country. Some of the songs were written by Christians in prison. We remembered these circumstances as we sang."

Children also participated in worship. Christian parents in Barnaul had demanded this right if their church were to register as the government ordered. "Like we adults, our children also wanted to bring their gifts of praise to Christ," one mother explains. "Often the children would memorize Gospel poems and readings, and they considered it a great privilege to recite these during the meeting."

In the crowded houses where they met, the congregation frequently stood during the entire service—two to four hours. However, if there were places to sit on the backless wooden benches, the *babushki* were given the first choice. During the service, the worshipers who were

*In 1968 the AUCECB began a theological correspondence school which graduated less than 200 students over its first eight years. This limited enrollment has given little opportunity for the tens of thousands of lay preachers across the Soviet Union who want to study. Pastors from unregistered churches are not allowed to enroll at all.

sitting changed places quietly with those who stood.

But during prayer the Christians always stood or knelt. "For a human ruler we show respect," a *babushka* who has been a Christian since the days of the tsar explains. "When we talk to the King of the universe, we must stand or kneel."

In Barnaul when the pastor announced a time for prayer, all who wanted to pray had an opportunity—and there were many. Mothers pled for their children facing atheistic hostility at school. Someone always remembered members of the body in prison for the sake of Christ. Prayer was offered for the church in the West—that it might be purified and strengthened.

While one person prayed aloud, a sea of prayer surged through the room as other believers whispered their petitions and praise, *"Da, Gospodi*–Yes, Lord, hear our prayer."

Almost before one person finished, another started to pray. When the last prayer was offered, soft singing rose from the worshipers to a crescendo of praise. "So many times we were discouraged and downcast," a mother of six remembers. "During those times of prayer, we felt the Holy Spirit come and comfort us. We rose from our knees strengthened and encouraged."

Christian meetings all over Russia customarily included a time for *privety* (greetings). One Sunday in Barnaul, Aleksandr K., a Christian visiting from the city of C., stood at the close of the meeting. "Greetings to you in the name of the Lord Jesus Christ from the believers in C.," he began in customary fashion. Then Aleksandr told about the pastor from his church who was "now in bonds." The listeners understood and silently prayed for the pastor in prison. Aleksandr described the man in the church in C. who had "turned from his sin and come back

55

to Christ." Again they understood that an informer had repented.

As members of Christ's body, believers in Barnaul wanted to obey Scriptural admonitions to give tithes and offerings to God. But these had to be gathered and distributed carefully. The Soviet government outlaws benevolent activities by nongovernment agencies, insisting that in a socialist society such activities are outmoded. Theoretically, the government handles all social assistance and strictly prohibits relief by religious organizations. Article 17 of Stalin's 1929 Law on Religious Associations explicitly states, "It is forbidden to render material assistance to other members."

Offerings were taken anyway. The Christians did not pass a basket, but everyone knew which deacons had been appointed to receive offerings. Unobtrusively, believers handed their gifts to these men, who shared them with needy members of the body.

Sometimes they used these offerings to pay fines levied for holding church meetings in their homes. Money was allocated to support families whose relatives were in prison for their faith. Evangelists who had given up their work to travel full-time and preach the Gospel also received support.

Although unregistered Christians in Barnaul were not officially allowed to organize as a church, they did anyway, choosing evangelists, deacons, and presbyters. They elected a chief presbyter, Dmitrii Vasilevich Miniakov, a soft-spoken, kindly man with Christian character as solid as Siberian ice.

In addition to the preachers, some men were ordained as deacons or general helpers in the church. The congregation expected these men to have good command of their own families and also be willing to give generously of their time to help other church members. Besides these duties, the preachers and deacons all held full-time jobs.

Traveling evangelists particularly infuriated the Soviet government. Although the Christians were willing and able to support them, the government insisted that these Christian workers were "parasites" because they did not have full-time jobs.

Russian evangelists followed their calling at great cost. They knew they could expect the police to trail them constantly, and often they could not live at home. When a man gave himself to become an evangelist, church members provided money and food for him and his family.

One of the deacons might arrive at the doorstep of the evangelist's apartment with a sack of potatoes and a bushel of *shchavel* (tart spinach). "Here is your family's food for the weekend," he would say. "You go to the next village, care for the believers there, and conduct communion for them this Sunday. We will look after your family."

Christians also took turns observing the evangelist's house to see if it was being watched by the police. Sometimes the evangelist could return home only at night and climb through a back window or door, careful to evade neighbors primed to report to the police. Before the sun rose, he knew he must move on again.

One Barnaul evangelist, Brother Igor, was so sought by the police that he did not dare return for months at a time. The Christians tried to arrange for him to meet his family at the homes of other believers. But even with this precaution, the attempt proved risky.

Weary of eluding the police and desperately lonely to see his family, Igor arrived in Barnaul one night in September. He walked four miles to his apartment and slipped inside the door. His wife's eyes filled with fear. "Only a few minutes ago the police were here inside the apartment looking for you. You must have passed them on the street." She tearfully embraced her husband. Igor stayed for a few hours and left before dawn.

Although life was especially grueling for evangelists, every day was difficult for all Russian believers in Barnaul. How did they react to pressure? "We learned to depend strongly on prayer. At every meeting we prayed, and on Wednesday night we met specifically to pray," one of the deacons recalls.

"During times of trouble we placed extra emphasis on prayer. For example, once when one of our members was arrested, we determined to pray for him as a church every three hours. Wherever we were—at work or at school—we prayed silently in the Spirit. It seemed to us that no one in the world knew or cared about our problems but God. We decided we must turn to him every three hours to find comfort, strength, and direction.

"Our church in Barnaul and churches all over Russia decided to designate every Friday as a day of prayer and fasting. We were comforted to know that on that day the sacrifice of prayer and praise was being offered to the God of heaven from every corner of our atheistic country."

Wednesday night prayer services were the most intimate of the meetings in Barnaul. The Christians did not invite guests to these meetings and also hoped the police would leave them in peace. When they felt certain they were among only their own members, they opened their hearts.

On a typical Wednesday night, a lay pastor read from Scripture to open the meeting. Then he asked a practical question, "Brothers and sisters, what needs do we have among us? Let us stand and make these known."

One man rose heavily to his feet. "I lost my temper this week at home in the presence of some nonbelievers, and I need your help." The Christians paused immediately to pray for their brother.

"Are there other needs?" the preacher asked quietly. Unashamedly, the believers confessed the weaknesses, problems, and temptations they had met that week. Openly, they asked the other members for advice and prayer.

In most Baptist churches in Russia, the first Sunday of every month was set aside for Communion—a sacrament Russian believers revere deeply and often prepare for by fasting the day before. On Communion Sundays in Barnaul, the participants stood to share the unleavened loaf of bread and chalice of wine that the deacons reverently passed from one person to the next. After the Communion service, the Christians greeted each other with a "holy kiss."

According to the Scriptures in I Corinthians 11, each Christian searched his heart before Communion. Those who felt an obstacle to partaking in Communion remained seated. After the service, the presbyter immediately counseled with any believer who did not participate. If two Christians had quarreled, they discussed their disagreement and promptly resolved it. "In our circumstances we could not afford disruption and disunity," one of the pastors explains. "We had to maintain purity and close-knit fellowship at all times."

Not surprisingly, non-Christians noticed the *sobornost*–the true spirit of community, love, and unity among believers in Barnaul. Neighbors living near Christian families remarked about how "the *veruiushchie* care for each other"—a compassion in marked contrast

59

to the mores of communist society.

After work, the believers visited the sick, befriended unbelievers, and visited Christian families who had relatives in prison. One seriously ill atheist agitator whom the Christians visited regularly admitted ruefully, "You believers don't leave the dying without comfort. That is your secret. My own comrades haven't visited me once. And you always bring gifts along besides!"

In Barnaul one curious woman asked her Christian neighbor, "Why are you Christians always so poor?"

The woman replied, "When we are poor, that means we have to help one another—that we are needed. If we all had everything we need, there would be no more opportunity to share, and we would lose that blessing."

Barnaul Christians did not expect to be self-sufficient. They even considered self-sufficiency a misfortune. "In our church when one person was in trouble, we all stood with him," Katia C., a practical woman in her forties, explains. "We never tried to escape another person's difficulties. Instead they bound us together and built up our faith. We expected to care for each other. We Christians are a family."

1. I. Grebtsov, "Once Upon A Time There Was A Little Girl," *Sovietskaia Rossiia* (Soviet Russia), Moscow, January 13, 1968. (Translated in *Religion in Communist Dominated Areas*, Vol. VII, Nos. 19, 20, October 15/31, 1968, p. 189.)

4

Witnessing, Barnaul Style

LENIN'S 1918 CONSTITUTION recognized "the right to religious and antireligious propaganda for all citizens."

Under Stalin, Lenin's constitution was changed. The right to antireligious propaganda was kept, but the right to religious propaganda was trimmed to "freedom of religious worship" in the 1936 constitution.

In practice, this law means that people may freely propagate atheism across the Soviet Union. Christians, however, face severe restrictions to sharing their faith. The Soviet government expects to contain all evangelistic activities within the approximately five thousand registered churches across Russia.

Article 125 of the U.S.S.R. constitution guarantees "freedom of assembly, including the holding of mass meetings and freedom of street processions and demonstrations." However, Russian Christians cannot organize evangelistic crusades. They cannot legally conduct Sunday schools, youth camps, or any other Christian youth activities. They are permitted only token printings of Christian literature and are warned not to listen to Christian broadcasts from foreign nations.

But all the laws and edicts that atheistic officials have

promulgated to stamp out the church—or at least prevent it from growing—have not stifled the Russian believers' witness.

They witness consistently through their daily life-style. For example, a Communist Party commission investigating why Christians are so successful in spreading their faith came to the following conclusions:

1. The believers are skillful, conscientious workers without exception and are respected for this.
2. The believers do not have problems with alcohol. Increasingly they are given tasks that require reliability.
3. The believers do not let anyone die without comfort.
4. The believers do not subscribe to any peace resolutions in world politics, but they do promote peace in the way they live. They live in peace with their families and also help other families when these families are having problems.[1]

Galina N. and her husband Lev, who have nine children, believe that witnessing begins inside the Christian family. "Within our families we have more freedom than anywhere else, and this is where our evangelistic outreach starts," Galina says. "In Russia it is now the fashion to have one or two children, but most of us Christians from Barnaul have six to ten children. We believe God blesses us with children so that we can strengthen and preserve the church.

"This does not mean we forget to witness to those outside our family. But this has to be done carefully."

Story after story has come from Barnaul to illustrate the many ways Christians there share their faith.

Andrei T. happened to discover a painting of Christ and John the Baptist with the inscription "Behold the Lamb of God" in a Barnaul art museum. Andrei regularly visited the museum, and when visitors stopped to study the painting, he offered to explain the inscription. His witness was so effective that exasperated officials eventually removed the painting from the museum.

Sometimes Christians ingeniously arranged situations to witness to strangers. One day Anatolii Y. was traveling on the train from Barnaul to another city with his friend Pavel R. They sat side by side in the crowded compartment.

After the train had pulled away from the station, Anatolii casually turned to Pavel. "Pavel Ivanovich, you say you believe in God. How can you believe in a God you cannot see?" While Anatolii continued the conversation as if he were not a believer, Pavel thoroughly explained the Gospel to him as the other passengers in the compartment listened. Some joined the discussion.

Yurii I. recalls an instance when he took the train from Barnaul to Novosibirsk with a group of several Christians. One of the Christians began to softly play hymns on his *balalaika* (Russian mandolin). *"Ochen prüatno*–it is very pleasant," one of the passengers said. "Why don't you play louder?"

The young man played the hymn through. Then softly he began to sing the words, "Christ is searching for you to bring you to your heavenly Father. . . ." One by one the other Christians joined the singing. The passengers listened closely. Several asked questions about the words of the hymn.

One day another Christian, Petr K., was riding the bus from Barnaul to another city just a few days before Easter. The passengers in his compartment enthusiastically exchanged plans for celebrating the holiday.

They debated the best method for coloring Easter eggs in traditional Ukrainian patterns. Eventually they talked about the holiday itself. Petr joined the discussion. "It's

some sort of religious holiday," one of the women specu-
lated. Petr agreed and then went on to tell her about the
meaning of Easter.

Dmitrii P., a grizzled old man who had endured the
hardships of Stalin's labor camps, was known for his bold
witness.

One afternoon Dmitrii and Yakov L., another believer,
were seated in the second-class "hard-seat" section of a
train. A third man, his face forlorn, sat across from them
in the compartment. Dmitrii, who owned a Bible, opened
it and softly read aloud. The man across the aisle closed
his newspaper and listened attentively.

He turned to Dmitrii. "What difficult days we live in,"
he sighed. "Children won't listen to their parents. There
is so much disobedience. It looks like the whole world is
coming to an end."

"It is!" Dmitrii exclaimed happily, turning pages of his
Bible to the Book of Revelation. Even though two other
passengers had entered the compartment, Dmitrii did
not stop speaking to the man across the aisle. The other
passengers could not help hearing as Dmitrii told the
man about Christ's Second Coming to earth.

When Dmitrii and Yakov stepped off the train, they
noticed the last man who had come into the compartment following them. He strode closer. "You are under
arrest," he snapped, showing them his KGB card. He
pointed straight ahead. "Now you will come with me."

The police at the station searched the two believers
thoroughly. Dmitrii clutched his Bible, but a policeman
snatched it from his hand. Yakov tried to take the blame.
"Please arrest me and let Dmitrii go—he is an old man,"
he pled.

But the police shoved both men into a cold cell where
other prisoners sat hunched like shadows. Although it

was winter and the cement floor was frigid, the two Christians knelt and prayed aloud. "Thank you, God, for leading us," Dmitrii prayed. Then the two sang hymns.

"Why don't you keep quiet?" the guard on patrol snarled.

A drunk who was drowsing in the corner awoke from his stupor at the singing. "Well, you really got yourself into trouble this time, didn't you?" he taunted.

"Maybe the Lord brought us here," Dmitrii smiled. "Maybe our great God brought us into prison just so we could tell you about him." Dmitrii walked over and sat beside the man. "But I must tell you about him quickly because we will only be staying here as long as he wants us to. In fact, I believe God will release us tonight!"

At one-thirty that morning the guard clanked open the prison cell door. "You're released!" he shouted to the two Christians while the other prisoners watched in speechless stupefaction. The drunk man stumbled after the two Christians as they walked from the cell door.

But the police decided to question the believers once more before releasing them. The guard ushered the men into a tight, gray office. "Are you going to preach anymore in railroad cars?" a stern KGB officer demanded.

"Of course we will as we have opportunity," Dmitrii answered honestly. "Who are we to obey—you or God?"

At three-thirty that morning the KGB finally thrust the two men out of the police station.

As the bold believers of Barnaul witnessed, people were converted to Christ. "Some remained secret believers," Nikolai V., one of the lay pastors, explains. "These people were like Joseph of Arimathea in the Bible. If a person held a high position, the cost of becoming a Christian was very great."

Many, however, paid the price and openly joined the

believers' ranks. In April, 1962, Yurii Ivanovich Mikhal-kov became a Christian at age 25. An engineer who had been raised through the Komsomol, he had worked at a well-paying job at Barnaul's machine factory. Yurii's tall stature matched his strong Christian witness, and immediately he began to share the Gospel with everyone he met—even the educated engineers around him.

Yurii had always been a meek person, not prone to talk about himself. That trait did not change, but Yurii became a bold conversationalist—about his faith in Christ.

One day, riding home from the university on a streetcar packed with young people, Yurii held out a new Bible. "I've discovered a good book," he announced to the students, who he knew were avid readers.

The young people crowded for a closer look. "Everybody has problems," Yurii continued. "This book has the solution to all of them. . . ."

Often Yurii used funerals as an occasion to witness. In fact, other Christians said, "Funerals are Yurii's specialty!"

At one funeral, a mourner sighed to Yurii, "Well, it's the end of everything."

"It's just the opposite. It's only the beginning!" Yurii replied, turning the conversation to eternal life.

With his engineer's aptitude for exactness, Yurii accurately chronicled persecutions of believers in his city. He used shorthand to transcribe the trials of Christians.

Soon after his conversion, Yurii's commitment to Christ was severely tested. His brother, a Communist Party member and a surgeon, excoriated Yurii for "turning from science to Christianity." Then other Communist Party members prodded Yurii's wife, a student in medical school, to try to force her husband to renounce his faith. Yurii refused. Finally she divorced him, moved to Moscow with their child, and remarried. Even after this Yurii implored his wife to return, but she refused.

Marina K. was another educated person who became a believer. A psychotherapist in her early thirties, she had been an ardent atheist. She was converted through the witness of believers in Barnaul. After her conversion, Marina followed the Christian faith as firmly as she had clung to communism.

Marina's conversion outraged officials at the hospital where she worked. "You—an educated person—allying yourself with those ignorant, fanatical Christians!" they cried. Through weekly indoctrination sessions, the officials tried to make Marina's philosophy conform again to communism. When they could not, they dismissed her from her job. Soon after that, her husband, angry and embarrassed at the disgrace of a *veruiushchaia* wife, deserted her.

In Barnaul, Vladimir Firsov, who worked at a communist social club, was converted to Christ. He had been raised as a Christian by his devout mother, but had turned from the faith. Soon after he became director of the communist club, Vladimir's wife died, leaving him to care for their eighteen-month-old daughter.

Grieved by his wife's death, he started to attend the Christian house meetings and also began to listen to Christian broadcasts from missionary stations in the West. He returned to God and was baptized in 1962.

After leaving his job as director of the communist club, Vladimir found his testimony as a Christian followed him and closed other jobs to him. Eventually, he became one of the evangelists in the church at Barnaul.

In another Siberian city, a communist director of a *kolkhoz* (collective farm) fiercely persecuted the Christians who worked under him. He personally disrupted their worship services and oversaw the arrest of some believers. For his fervor as a Communist Party member he received the Order of Lenin decoration.

In the process of interrogating and persecuting the Christians, the *kolkhoz* director gradually heard the Gospel. When he condemned the Christians, they often replied with Bible verses. Slowly the Scriptures changed the director's heart.

One day he accompanied a group of *druzhinniki* to disband a meeting. But at the door he discovered he could not bludgeon the believers. Instead, he fell on his knees in front of the startled Christians and cried to God for salvation.

After his conversion he personally went to every Christian he had persecuted to ask forgiveness. He traveled to the Communist Party headquarters in Barnaul and turned in his Communist Party card. "I belong to the Christians now," he resolutely announced.

Angrily, the authorities accepted the card. "If you persist in your foolish Christianity, we will strip away your awards," they threatened, confident that the loss of pension which accompanies awards would persuade the director to renounce his faith. Eventually the director did lose his pension and position, but did not deny his faith.

Nadia and Vasilii S., who lived in Barnaul, had turned away from the Christian faith, although both had attended church as children. They had lived in tiny, crowded apartments all their lives. More than anything else they wanted a house of their own.

But building a house in the Soviet Union is a staggering task. Building supplies are scarce and expensive. Like many other Soviet citizens, Vasilii and Nadia started to steal supplies. They resorted to bribes to obtain materials they could not buy. But as their dream house slowly materialized, their happiness seemed to crumble.

They started to take time off from their housebuilding on Sunday to attend Christian meetings in a nearby home. At first they stood outside listening to the service through the door. Then they crept inside but stood at the farthest corner.

One Sunday, even before the lay preacher had finished his sermon, Vasilii and his wife stumbled down the aisle. They fell to their knees before the Christians. With tears Vasilii asked God's forgiveness and pled with the church to pray for him.

Even though evangelistic altar calls are forbidden by the Soviet government, sinners who wanted to repent often came to the front anyway. The police could not accuse pastors of issuing public invitations when sinners came forward by themselves at the urging of the Holy Spirit.

After prayer, the believers customarily asked the new convert, "Have you found forgiveness? Have you found the joy of the Lord in your heart? What have you received from God now that you have repented?"

Often the joyful congregation started to sing while the new convert knelt at the front. "A Wandering Sheep Has Been Found" was a frequent choice.

Among Russian Christians, conversion is invariably followed by baptism. In the Soviet Union both Christians and Communist Party officials recognize baptism as a significant occasion symbolizing a sincere change.

The Soviet government views baptism as the final step of a person's commitment to Christianity. In an article entitled "Sectarian Pedagogy and Soviet Law," one Soviet government spokesman wrote about the meaning of baptism among Evangelical Christians-Baptists:

> Baptism is a conscious act, and signifies not simply conver-
> sion . . . but the public token of the convert's acceptance as a
> member of the church, with all the ensuing obligations.
> Quite obviously, this vital step in life is particularly mean-
> ingful for a young mind. Not merely by chance many teen-
> age high-school students literally change before one's eyes
> after baptism. They no longer watch films, no longer
> socialize with classmates, and so on.[2]

Because of the great significance of this Christian sacrament, the Soviet government consistently discourages
any baptisms and specifically forbids baptisms of citizens
under eighteen. At one point in the early 1960s some
officials insisted that the minimum age for baptism
should be thirty. After all, they argued, wasn't that the
age at which Christ himself had been baptized?

In their campaign to curtail baptisms of children
among Orthodox believers, some Soviet officials soberly
asserted, "Baptisms are a health hazard." According to a
1970 Soviet government pamphlet entitled "Children
and Religion: A Memorandum for Parents,"

> Statistics are impartial. Studies carried out by doctors show:
> —that one child out of ten gets seriously ill after the chris-
> tening ceremony (most frequently with an inflammation of
> the lungs or middle ear).
> —that the general rate of illness among christened children
> is twice as high as among those not christened.
> —that these ceremonies are sometimes the cause of out-
> breaks of infectious disease among children. For example,
> in the village of Perovka in Orenburg Province, an epidemic
> of scarlatina broke out as a result of mass christening.
> —that there have been instances of drownings of little ones
> in baptismal fonts.[3]

Often local authorities tried to break up baptismal

meetings ahead of time. For example, on one occasion several believers from Barnaul planned to attend the baptism of five new converts in the small town of S. When officials in S. heard about the proposed baptismal service, they correctly calculated that delegations of Christians from other towns would attend. Hastily they imposed a quarantine on the town.

When the Christians arrived at the train station in S., they were swiftly turned back. "The city is quarantined—only emergency cases can go through," the *militsiia* sternly announced.

Efrim L.'s cousin was being baptized, and he was determined to attend. "I'm going to help bury a dead man," Efrim told the guard, remembering the Apostle Paul's description of baptism. Stiffly the guard waved Efrim through the quarantine checkpoint.

Russian Christians carefully prepare new converts for baptism. Often there is a year of probation before a new convert is baptized, although this requirement varies from one congregation to another. During that time other believers watch and encourage the new convert and instruct him in doctrine and Christian living.

Christians frankly discuss the cost of following Christ in Russia with the new believer: "Are you prepared for persecution? Will you be able to stand true to Christ if only you alone are left? If you are questioned by the police and asked to inform on your brothers and sisters, will you be able to withstand pressure?" Finally, members vote whether to accept the candidate for baptism. The decision must be unanimous.

During times of persecution Russian believers have been forced to baptize new converts in secret. Christians in Barnaul recall baptismal services at 4:00 A.M. when believers gathered on the edge of the city at the Ob River to witness the baptisms of new converts as they joined hands and stepped into the water.

But Russian believers much prefer to perform baptism openly and outdoors. Outside, passersby notice the converts in their white gowns. Curious, they linger to see what is happening and hear the Gospel preached as each new convert speaks his testimony before he is baptized. In this way baptismal services—which are permitted by law even though they are sometimes illegally prevented—become a means of mass evangelism.

Sometimes baptismal services are held in winter. In Barnaul, this means that the preacher must chop a hole in the thick ice. Valentina Y., who was baptized in November, remembers her baptism vividly. The Christians gathered for the service near a lake outside the city. Snow had already fallen. The deacons chopped a hole through the ice, and Valentina and two other young converts were baptized while the lay pastor stood for half an hour in the freezing water. "But none of us caught a cold," Valentina recalls with a smile.

1. Winrich Scheffbauch, *Christians Under the Hammer and Sickle,* Zondervan, 1974, p. 122.

2. I. Brazhnik, "Sectarian Pedagogy and Soviet Life," *Nauka i Religiia* (Science and Religion), No. 6, Moscow, June, 1971, pp. 36-39. (Translated in *Religion in Communist Dominated Areas,* Vol. XII, Nos. 7, 8, and 9, July-August-September, 1973, p. 120.)

3. "Children and Religion: A Memorandum for Parents," 1970. Printing ordered by the Ministry of Public Health. (Translated in *Religion in Communist Dominated Areas,* Vol. XII, Nos. 1, 2, and 3, January-February-March, 1973, p. 34.)

5

To Jail

THE REOPENING OF the prayer house on Christmas Eve, 1962, was not, as might have been hoped, a government signal for detente with the Christians. Throughout the summer and fall, harassment had been on the increase as the *militsiia* strove to gather incriminating evidence against the unregistered Baptists.

Finally, on December 27, the presbyter of the church, Dmitrii Miniakov, was arrested and jailed. Five other men of the congregation were questioned the same day and had their homes searched.

On December 29, two of the five were picked up: Grigorii Lebedev and Yurii Mikhalkov, the young engineer who had been a believer since April. All were charged with organizing harmful religious meetings under Article 227 of the RSFSR penal code. This harsh law, enacted the year before, states:

Organizing or directing a group, the activity of which, carried on under the appearance of preaching religious beliefs and performing religious ceremonies, is connected with causing harm to citizens' health or with any other infringements of the person or rights of citizens, or with inducing citizens to refuse social activity or the performance of civic duties, or with drawing minors into such a group, shall be punished by deprivation of freedom for a term not exceeding five years or by exile by a similar term with or without confiscation of property.

On New Year's Eve, several Barnaul believers visited the office of the procurator of the October Region. They asked where the Christian prisoners were being detained and why. The officials answered by herding the Christians out of the office and assigning fifteen-day sentences to Artur Shtertser, M. Dik, and others.

But the case did not come to trial until the next May, by which time the number of defendants had grown to five—the presbyter Miniakov, Lebedev, Mikhalkov, Shtertser, and Iosif Budimir. The location for the trial was the "Red Corner" of a factory, which had a large hall used as a court. Newspaper articles and radio and television broadcasts slandered the believers. Posters caricaturing Christians were hung in public places.

Soviet citizens are legally allowed to attend public trials. However, officials persistently attempted to prevent members of the Barnaul congregation from entering the Red Corner.

Across the Soviet Union, police have devised several tactics to stop believers from attending the trials of fellow Christians. In many instances they hold the trials in unannounced locations. Other times they begin the trial and then suddenly postpone it or move it to another location. Sometimes the trial is purposely conducted late at night.

During the five-day trial of the Barnaul believers, police barred Christians from entering the front door of the courtroom, which held about 500 people. "There is no more room," they lied. They forcibly turned away local Christians as well as believers who had traveled across Russia just to support their suffering brothers.

Finally, some of the Christians discovered a back door to the courtroom through which the police had ushered in Communist Party members, *Komsomoltsy,* journalists, and other observers. One Christian unobtrusively became friends with a journalist and got inside. Another carried a copy of the communist *Agitator* magazine in his hand and was waved into the courtroom.

When the trial began and the five defendants saw that many of their Christian friends had not been admitted, they bravely protested. "Since you have not allowed our friends to attend this public trial, as they are legally permitted, we are not going to answer your questions," they told the judge. "When you allow our friends to enter and witness the proceedings against us, then we will cooperate."

Some of the observers inside the courtroom sided with the defendants. "It is a public trial," they said. "Their friends have a right to attend."

To forestall further commotion, the judge reluctantly allowed more of the Christians inside the courtroom. Those who stood outside kept a prayer vigil. When the defendants were marched to the platform, the believers in the audience stood to show their solidarity with their brothers. They shouted to the five men, "Greetings to you brethren on behalf of your freedom!" And then, the five men knelt and prayed aloud.

Like all Soviet citizens, the five Christians could have chosen the services of a government defense lawyer. They declined this dubious assistance, citing Article 146 of the penal code which states, "If a person is mentally balanced, he has the right to conduct his own defense."

"Christ and the truth are our defense," the five Barnaul believers told the judge.

They had made a point of being familiar with Soviet laws. The judge and procurator (prosecution lawyer) listened in confusion as Yurii Mikhalkov quoted clauses from the 1918 decree on the separation of church, state, and school, the 1929 law on religious associations, and the Soviet constitution adopted in 1936.

The five men also constantly quoted Scripture, which they considered their best defense. Meanwhile, the communist officials tried to prove that Christian activities such as preaching were in fact "slanderous fabrications discrediting the Soviet political and social order."

The five defendants answered firmly. One spoke for all when he said, "We are grateful that we stand before you today not as criminals. We stand before you as Christians who believe in Jesus Christ and trust in God. We wish that all of you would have the same faith and joy that we do."

One of the Christians explains, "While our brethren on trial for their faith quoted God's Word and preached, we prayed God would give them power. The courtroom was packed with atheists. Our five brethren thanked God for the opportunity to sow the seed. We knew the whole city was talking about the trial."

The five were eventually sentenced to serve from two to five years of general and strict regime* in the Barnaul

*In the Soviet Union, prison sentences are classified according to the following degrees of severity:

General regime–one visit and one food parcel allowed every three months. A monthly allowance is given to buy food in the camp shop. No restriction on mail.

Reinforced regime–After serving half their sentence, prisoners are allowed one food parcel and one visitor every six months. They are allowed one visit to the camp shop every three months and two letters a year.

Strict regime–A food and clothing parcel and one letter are allowed once a prison. The courts also fined several other Christians. Yevgenii Bever received a fine deducting twenty-five percent of his wages for six months. T. F. Kiriachkov was fined fifty rubles. P. I. Klimontov had to pay twenty-five percent of his wages for one month.

It is estimated that at any given time since 1961, approximately 150 Baptists from unregistered churches across the U.S.S.R. have been in jail. Sometimes Christians have gone to jail for a few days or weeks as a warning. Other believers have been sentenced to compulsory labor and forced to work for drastically reduced wages. In some instances, extended fines have been deducted from a believer's salary—a sentence often meted to pregnant women or to Christians with physical infirmities.

In other instances, Christians have lost their jobs or their permission to attend university. For example, on January 20, 1963, Yevgenii Bever was expelled from the Altai Agricultural Institute in his third year because of his religious convictions.

The following year, Irina T., who worked as a nurse's aide, was discharged as a punishment for helping to conduct Sunday schools. She was assigned to sweep and shovel streets—a job she was forced to accept to help support her family of ten children.

"It was hard work," Irina recalls, "and a job that most people didn't want. In Siberia so much snow falls that it's difficult to find a place to pile it after a while. But my

year. One visit is permitted every year after half the sentence is served.

Special regime–one letter every year and one visit annually after half the sentence is served. No food parcels are allowed.

The camp diet contains approximately one third of the calories vital to health.

street-sweeping job had compensations. I was assigned a section and worked alone. No one harassed me or tried to demote me because I was a believer.

"A few years later I was finally permitted to find another job. My boss said he was sorry to see me leave. 'I guess our division won't take first prize for street sweeping anymore now that you're gone,' he said."

6

Children of God

Younger members of the sect are obliged to spend not less than 10-20 hours a week praying, closing their eyes and folding their hands on their chest. . . .

The "criticism" of science and atheism is one of the most favored themes in Baptist sermons. Their authors strive to prove that science is supposedly powerless in cracking the inner laws of the universe and that science "describes" more or less reliably only the outer manifestations of nature. . . .

In this way, quite a detailed and well-thought-out system of spiritual robbery and enslavement of young people ensues. And here is the result: their outlook is found to be incredibly narrow and impoverished. . . . [1]

The Soviet government has rigorously attempted to curb Christian parents, whom they accuse of subjecting their children to religious fanaticism. The article excerpted above, entitled "Hunters of Children's Souls," asserted that the sight of Christian children "stirred feelings of profound compassion and at the same time feelings of outrage against those who had brought them to this condition." According to the Soviet writer, the children "looked beaten, slack-jawed, permeated with the fear of 'God Almighty,' and their statements bore overtones of a wholly unchildlike hatred toward all that is 'worldly.'"

The Stefan Kuznetsovs,* a Christian family who lived in Barnaul but have now immigrated to West Germany, would describe the situation of Christian families quite differently.

In Barnaul, Stefan and Anna lived in a tiny three-room apartment with their six children. Beside their stove, eight pairs of shoes stood in neat stair-step arrangement. Around the walls of the two front rooms were single beds used as couches by day, each covered with a lacy spread. The biggest bed was for three children, who slept width-wise.

Besides the two living/bedrooms, there was a narrow kitchen and a tiny room with a shower and toilet. Each room had a door to try to provide some privacy in cramped space. Anna and Stefan had no telephone or washing machine. They considered themselves fortu-nate to own a small refrigerator (their first) and a two-burner stove.

Like most Christian families in Russia, the Kuznetsovs hung a Scripture plaque in their front room. "This way other Christians knew immediately that we were believ-ers," Anna explains. "Also, the plaque often opened a way to witness to nonbelievers."

Stefan earned 125 rubles a month working in a tractor factory; Anna earned 90 rubles as a janitor in a nursery school. Since their family was large, the Kuznetsovs re-ceived a small monthly allowance from the state for each child. They paid only 15 rubles a month for their apart-ment. Medical care and education were free.

However, food and clothing were expensive for a fam-ily of eight. A man's suit, for example, cost about 100

*pseudonym

rubles. Nevertheless, each of Anna and Stefan's six children had at least one change of clothes besides their school uniforms. The girls had colored ribbons to weave into their braids on school days and white ribbons for church. Each child owned one pair of shoes and a pair of simple slippers worn inside the apartment to conserve the shoes and the few woven rugs scattered around the floors.

The Kuznetsovs didn't complain about their crowded conditions. Some larger families lived in even fewer rooms. And Anna and Stefan were thankful for the small garden plots outside the city that Stefan's factory allowed its workers to use.

Anna and Stefan struggled a long time with the Soviet state over the souls of their children. The Kuznetsovs knew that Stalin's 1929 laws on religion restricted youth from joining any religious organization until age 18. They also were aware that the 1960 Letter of Instructions to presbyters prohibited children from even accompanying their parents to worship services. These restrictions and others contained in the Letter of Instructions and New Statutes were some of the reasons Anna and Stefan did not return to the registered church.

In 1962, when the five Christian leaders from Barnaul went to prison, Anna and Stefan knew that they had been charged under Article 227 of the penal code, one clause of which declares it illegal to entice minors to participate in religious activities "harmful to the health of citizens and encroaching upon the person or the right of individuals."

In 1966, a decree on religion issued by the Soviet government banned Sunday schools and informal religious instruction for minors. In a 1968 marriage and family law, restrictions were placed even on religious instruction given by parents to their own children, despite an earlier Soviet decree that proclaims, "Citizens can teach and be taught religion privately."

The 1968 law further stipulates that children may be removed from parents who exhibit antisocial behavior—a term Soviet courts sometimes interpret to include such actions as prohibiting children from joining communist clubs for youth. Russian Christians also do not permit their children to attend movies. They often go a strict step further and prohibit participation in sports, musical activities, or any social events outside the church. The Soviet state can claim final jurisdiction over children in cases like this, since a 1969 marriage and family law declares that parents have no ownership rights to their children. Children belong to society, and parents are entrusted with their custody by the state only so long as they fulfill obligations along proper ideological lines.*

But the Kuznetsovs refused to be intimidated. "The children must see that we parents are genuine and victorious in our faith," Stefan declares. "Here in our home they must learn that God is alive and powerful."

Anna adds, "As a family of eight living in three rooms, we could not afford quarreling. Christian unity and love begin at home, and we try to teach our children that. Even the youngest children know that if they squabble, they must kiss the person they have hurt and ask each other's forgiveness. When the children need it, we spank them—but not in anger. We have made it a rule always to pray with the children before and after the spanking."

Anna and Stefan were more fortunate than many

*All this is in contrast to the U.N.-sponsored Convention on the Fight Against Discrimination in the Field of Education, which the U.S.S.R. signed in 1965. Article 5 of this convention states: "Parents and, in appropriate cases, legal guardians, should have the possibility of insuring religious and moral education of their children according to their own convictions."

Christian families in the Soviet Union. They owned a Bible—a treasure they often shared with other Christian families. Even when the Bible was loaned out, their children memorized hand-copied portions of Scripture. Stefan often told them stories from the Old Testament— how God helped David slay an evil giant, or how he saved Daniel from the lions' den. "Just as Samuel's mother gave her child to God, we have also given you to God," the children were often told.

The Kuznetsovs listened daily to Christian radio broadcasts from missionary stations in the West. When the youngest child, Natasha, was four, she liked to wear her Sunday dress to listen because the programs made her feel like she was at church. The three youngest children considered Aunt Tania, who tells Bible stories on the broadcasts, to be a relative. "The children consider all the aunts and uncles in the church and also the radio speakers as part of the same family," Anna explains with a smile.

The Christian uncles and aunts are also the children's heroes. In Barnaul every Christian child in the unregistered congregation reveres Uncle Yurii Mikhalkov, the engineer who had received commendations for his good work. They know that Uncle Yurii has suffered to become a follower of Christ. The parents have explained to even the youngest children that "Uncle Yurii is sitting in prison now because he wanted everyone—even his friends at the university—to know about Jesus."

Anna and Stefan did not spare their children from biblical texts such as Philippians 1:29: "For unto you it is given in the behalf of Christ, not only to believe on him, but also to suffer for his sake."

"We had no time to read our children fairy tales," Anna says. "While they were still tiny, we were forced to teach them that Christians must expect to suffer. We had to train them how to reply if the authorities questioned them.

"Every day our children were taught atheism at school. Their teachers tried to persuade them to turn against Christianity. Sometimes they even asked the children to inform on other Christians. I had to tell my six-year-old Olga, 'If the authorities ask, you must not tell them that Sister Sonia is your Sunday school teacher. If you do, they may bring Sister Sonia to a trial, and because of your words they might throw her into prison.' "

All Christian education in Anna and Stefan's family was not sober, however. Stefan bought games for the children at *detskii magazin,* the children's store—and altered them toward Christian ends. The children hovered for hours over a game with a bulb that lights when the player matches the correct biblical character with the corresponding story in Scripture. Anna designed a coloring book by drawing pictures from Bible stories.

The parents also devised dramas to teach their children spiritual truths. Once Stefan brought a bundle of twigs inside the apartment. He handed the children one twig and asked them to break it. It snapped easily. As he added twigs, the bundle became harder to break—"just like the strength we will have if we stand together for Christ," Stefan told the children.

Another time Anna used thread for an object lesson. She wrapped a single thread around ten-year-old Katia's hand. The thread, Anna said, represented a small sin. A single thread seemed harmless, but as Anna wrapped more threads around Katia's hand the children saw the binding effects of even seemingly small sins.

Stefan and Anna also taught their children Christian songs; they sang with their family by the hour. Often when the whole family listened to the Christian radio broadcasts, they sang along with the familiar hymns. "If there is singing to God in a home, there is less room for the devil to tempt our children," Anna emphasizes.

In Russia the family is the first stronghold of Christian fellowship. However, believers in Barnaul determined that their children must also receive systematic Bible training with other Christian children outside their own family. They divided children into four groups, and adults and older teenagers from the church volunteered for the perilous assignment of teaching them. Usually the Sunday schools met after the Sunday morning services and at special times during the week.

One Sunday in February, the primary age group met at Anna and Stefan's apartment. The children bundled up in their long stockings and heavy coats after the morning service. Then four adults escorted them on the trolley car to the Kuznetsovs' apartment.

After they arrived, one of the older young people acted as sentry to alert the others if the police approached. In that case the children knew that they should immediately divide into small informal groups and scatter toys about the room. Anna prepared a lunch of rolls, boiled potatoes, cucumbers, pickles, and butter while another sister taught the lesson.

When they started conducting the Sunday schools in the early sixties, the Barnaul Christians had no written materials. Later, they painstakingly wrote and mimeographed Sunday school lessons, Scripture verses, and poems. This literature, however, has been continually confiscated by the police during house searches.

Although they rotated their Sunday schools from house to house and tried to meet as unobtrusively as possible, the police sometimes disrupted the meetings and cornered the frightened children. "What are you doing here? What have they told you? How often do you come?" they would ask.

One of the police complained to a Christian mother, "You've done a wonderful job teaching your children. They won't answer anything."

"We teach our children not to be like Judas," the mother replied tersely.

One Sunday the police halted a children's meeting in an apartment. A surly policeman asked a seven-year-old girl, "How do you know there is a God? Have you seen God?"

The little girl mused a moment and then answered, "The Bible says that only the pure in heart can see God. That's why we can see God and you can't."

Besides the Sunday schools held in homes, the adults in the Barnaul church planned another ingenious system of Christian education. Each week, the deacons assigned older young people and adults from the church to visit homes and conduct Christian training among the children of the family. The visitors took time to talk with each of the children, play games with them, and win their confidence.

Anna observes, "With such large families as most of us had, it was important that we planned specific times for Bible lessons. It helped the children sometimes to hear the Scripture lesson from someone outside their own family. This reinforced the teaching we gave them ourselves."

Atheistic officials considered special church holidays such as Easter especially corrupting for children. However, the *militsiia* assigned to attend church meetings could not help noticing how greatly the children enjoyed the Christian celebrations.

One Easter service the Christians in Barnaul hung a sign formed with colored lights on the door of their prayer house that said, *"Khristos voskres–Voistinu voskres!*—Christ is risen—truly he is risen!" During the four-hour meeting, many of the children recited poems and Scriptures. Afterwards the adults gave the children presents—*paskha* (a cheese dessert), *kulich* bread, hard-boiled eggs with brightly colored shells, wall mottoes, toys, and games. The festivity delighted the Christian children and also attracted neighborhood children.

In its attempt to stamp out religion, particularly among susceptible young people, the Soviet government has systematically initiated communist ceremonies and holidays intended to replace Christian ones such as Easter. Komsomol weddings are supposed to replace religious ones. Communist dedication of infants is calculated to take the place of baptisms, and communist coming-of-age ceremonies at age 16, when internal Soviet passports are issued, are organized to supplant such religious practices as confirmation. Ceremonies for consecration of workers and joining the Red Army are also encouraged by Soviet authorities so that secular rituals will become "an inalienable, integral part of the many-sided spiritual life of our society. These rituals should enable interaction among people . . . and of course they should serve as an active means of atheistic upbringing and training."[2]

The text of one "commemorative certificate" issued at an atheistic ceremony designed to replace baptism reads:

When you are grown, read these precepts and always follow them.

Remember that you are a citizen of the Great Motherland—the Union of Soviet Socialist Republics—the country of freedom and happiness, where man is a friend, comrade, and brother to man.

Guard the Motherland as the apple of your eye, increase her wealth and glory.

Walk firmly on the path of life indicated by the great Lenin. Be honorable, diligent, and orderly in great and small matters. Respect parents, elders. Support the honor of the collective in which you learn and labor.

Remember, fortune is joyful labor for the glory of one's people, the battle for the beautiful future of mankind—communism![3]

Many of the believers in Barnaul and in other churches throughout Russia are young. This increasing percentage of young people particularly annoys communist authorities. For example, the atheistic publication *Liudyna i Svit (Man and World)* insists, "Today's typical believer is elderly, usually female, has little education, is isolated from any sort of working collective, is a housewife, a pensioner, or a part-time worker in a *kolkhoz* or production plant. However, on a religious holiday, one may find an occasional minor, a young man, or a girl in a church or sectarian house of worship."[4]

The many Christian young people in Barnaul use birthday parties, graduations, and every possible celebration as an occasion for a Christian gathering. Seventeen-year-old Volodia B. says, with a smile, "In a youth group as large as ours, we can always find someone with a birthday."

Sometimes the meetings are unstructured, giving the young people a chance to sing, pray, and talk about God with other believers. Their closeness strongly compensates for the lack of a university education or promising career, which they probably will not receive unless they deny their faith.

At other times the young people carefully plan their meeting. A passage of Scripture is assigned. The young people in charge pass out slips of paper. On some are verses of Scripture which the person is asked to explain. On others the young people have written probing questions: "Do you have a grudge against anyone in the youth group?" "Are you seriously praying for our brothers and sisters in prison?" "Describe your conversion experience." "How many times a day do you pray?" "How do you overcome temptation?" Everyone receives a paper and everyone participates. At the end of the meeting, slips of paper with each other's names and names of unconverted friends are distributed as prayer reminders for the week.

Youth in Barnaul often plan gatherings with young Christians from other areas. Communist holidays such as International Labor Day (May 1), Day of Victory (May 9), and Revolution Day (November 7-8) are frequently used as opportunities to organize mass meetings for young people from registered and unregistered churches who come from hundreds of miles around Barnaul.

Once the unregistered churches from the Altai Territory planned a youth rally and obtained permission to use the registered church in the city of Novosibirsk. But more typically, the youth meetings are held in the forest. "There's more space, and the *militsiia* are less likely to disturb us," says Sergei R., an eighteen-year-old from Barnaul.

As many as eight hundred young people have attended these rallies in the forests of Siberia. The young people are careful to gather far enough into the forest that no one will accuse them of disrupting public peace. Nevertheless, such huge meetings sometimes attract the attention of the police. Sometimes they only record

„ *И вознесся дым фимиама с молитвами святых от руки Ангела пред Богом* " Откр. 8, 4.

Возлюбленные Господом братья и сестры Запада, с искренним приветствием обращаются сегодня к вам молодые христиане далекой Сибири.

Мы признательны Вам за вашу солидарность, чуткое внимание к нам, гонимым за Имя Иисуса Христа. Ваше письмо взволновало многие христианские круги молодежи и принесло большое благословение, чувствуя невидимую, но столь сильную поддержку, которую несут ваши искренние молитвы пред Богом. Наши молитвы не одиноки - они соединяются в единый могучий поток с вашими и, обретая великую силу, несутся в те благословенные чаши, что пред Престолом Бога. (Откр. 5, 8)

Радость наполняет наши сердца, видя, что в наших гонениях вы не остаетесь равнодушными, что мы не одни - с нами друзья, с которыми соединила нас кровь Иисуса.

Пусть голос наш слышит сегодня планета,
Пусть знает, что мы не умрём! –
Ведь с нами Христос Иисус с Назарета,
Ведь с нами друзья из далёкой страны!

Пусть наши взаимные деяния (наши страдания и лишения, а ваши молитвы) принесут и умножат плод пред Господом. "Впрочем, братья, радуйтесь, усовершайтесь, утешайтесь, будьте единомысленны, мирны, – и Бог любви и мира будет с вами" 2Кор.13,11.

Настанет уже вскоре то время, когда мы будем свидетелями тех истин, о которых пишет Иоанн в своём откровении и тогда, видя всю Славу Божию, не найдётся того, кто будет жалеть о времени, проведённом на коленях пред Господом, ибо каждый увидит, как воскурится фимиам с молитвами всех святых на золотом жертвеннике (Откр. 8,3)

Подвязавшись вместе с нами за истину, пусть и впредь не ослабевают ваши молитвы о всех святых и о нас.

Соединимся сегодня в единую христианскую семью, для которой нет границ, нет расстояний, – есть чистое, необъятное, лазурное небо, которое над вами и над нами – одно, где наш любимый Друг Иисус, и где мы вскоре встретимся у ног Его.

До встречи в небе, друзья!
– Молодые христиане Сибири!

names and threaten, while other times they push their way through the crowd with clubs until the meeting disperses.

Young people from Barnaul frequently travel to outlying areas in smaller groups to encourage other churches. One Saturday night twenty of them traveled to a small town where they planned to conduct a communion service the next morning.

On the way to the meeting the young people sang—so well that the conductor offered not to charge them for their train tickets. But the young people paid and continued singing. Two plain-clothes policemen disliked the music. When the youth group arrived in the city of B., they arrested the elderly preacher, Brother Petr, who had accompanied the group.

Inside the prison, Brother Petr refused to eat until he was released. The young people took turns standing vigil outside, patiently singing hymns. The police refused to allow the young people to conduct the communion service, but after seven days finally released Brother Petr.

In 1974 several young Christians from Barnaul sent the following letter to the West. They wrote:

> Dear brothers and sisters in the West, beloved in the Lord, we young Christians of far eastern Siberia greet you this day.
>
> We are obliged to you for your solidarity and concerned attention to us as we are being persecuted for the name of Jesus Christ. . . . We feel the invisible but strong support of your sincere prayers before God. Our prayers are not alone—they are united in one mighty stream with yours and, gaining great strength, flow into those blessed bowls which stand before God's throne (Revelation 5: 8).
>
> Joy fills our hearts when we see that you do not remain indifferent to our persecution, and that we are not alone—

we have friends with whom we are united by the blood of Jesus.

Let the world hear our voice this day.

Let it know that we are still alive!

Surely Christ Jesus of Nazareth is with us.

Surely friends from a distant country are with us!

Let our mutual concerns (our sufferings and deprivations, and your prayers) bear fruit before God. "Finally, brethren, farewell. Be perfect, be of good comfort, be of one mind, live in peace; and the God of love and peace shall be with you" (II Corinthians 13:11).

That time will come very soon when we shall witness those truths which John wrote about in his Revelation; then will we see all the glory of God. There will be no one who will grieve when brought to his knees before the Lord, for each will see incense offered with the prayers of all the saints upon the golden altar (Revelation 8:3).

Unite with us for the truth, and don't let your prayers for all the saints and for us grow weak in the future.

Let us unite today into one Christian family which knows neither border nor distance—only the pure, boundless, azure sky which lies above you and us. There is one sky, where our beloved Friend Jesus is, and where we will soon meet at his feet.

Until we meet in heaven, dear friends,

Young Christians of Barnaul, Siberia, U.S.S.R.

1. V. Andreyev and F. Filippov, "Hunters of Children's Souls," *Vospitanie* (Education), No. 1, Moscow, 1970, pp. 52, 53. (Translated in *Religion in Communist Dominated Areas*, Vol. IX, Nos. 21-22, November, 1970, pp. 188, 189.)

2. *Nauka i Religiia*, Vol. 12, 1975, p. 25.

3. N. Riabinskii, "New Times—New Rituals," *Sovetskie Profsoiuzy* (Soviet Trade Unions), No. 19, October, 1965. (Translated in *Religion in Communist Dominated Areas*, Vol. V, No. 3, February 15, 1966, p. 28.)

4. A. Yeryshev and P. Kosukha, "Instilling Irreconcilability," *Liudyna i Svit (Man and World)*, No. 2, Kiev, January, 1969. (Translated in *Religion in Communist Dominated Areas*, Volume VIII, Nos. 13-16; July-August, 1969, p. 135.)

7

Anatolii and Larisa

ANATOLII WAS TWELVE and Larisa eleven the year that the police locked the registered prayer house at 67 Radishchevskaia Street. Both were caught in the tumult that followed when their parents and others began to meet in homes for church services—the time when some Christians came to be called *Initsiativniki* (reformers).

Anatolii and Larisa had always been together in the group of children who gathered cautiously for Sunday school. As teenagers, they attended birthday parties that were really youth meetings and occasionally attended mass meetings in the forest. But carefully following the conservative customs of Christian courtship in Russia, they had never been together alone.

However, by the time Anatolii was twenty, he felt certain he loved Larisa and wanted to marry her. But he did not propose to Larisa directly. With traditional circumspection, he had never spoken to her except when the group of Christian young people was together.

On a blustery night in January, Anatolii called at the home of Grigorii M., a pastor of the Barnaul church whom all the young people trusted as their friend and spiritual advisor. "Brother Grigorii cares," the young people had remarked more than once.

Grigorii's wife Vera welcomed Anatolii into their three-room wooden house. She seemed perpetually patient, despite the commotion of her own six children and a stream of Christian brothers and sisters who constantly stopped to talk with the pastor.

"Ah, so it is Larisa," the pastor smiled.

Anatolii, his face flushed, finally said, "If it is God's will, I want to marry her, Brother Grigorii."

The pastor heartily approved the marriage. He had watched Anatolii and Larisa mature in Christian faith, and he had suspected their attraction to each other. "For the next three months I will pray with you," he said, trying to be heard above the children's choir practicing in the next room. "Then I will call on Larisa's parents."

Anatolii nodded. The procedures of courtship and marriage were clearly understood among all the Christian young people, even though seldom discussed. If Larisa's parents agreed, then he and the pastor would call together on Larisa. With a surge of joy, Anatolii felt certain Larisa would say yes.

In April, the pastor and Anatolii—a nervous suitor—stood by the apartment door of Larisa's family. Larisa herself answered their knock. Her long auburn hair swept gently from her forehead. The crimson of her cheeks and excitement in her eyes seemed to Anatolii hopeful signs, although she shyly summoned her father as soon as the guests were inside the door.

"But it is to you we must speak now, Larisa," the pastor said with a smile. "Do you feel it is God's will for you to marry Anatolii? Would you like some time to pray over your decision?"

Next Sunday the pastor announced the news. A ripple

of whispers passed through the section where the *babushki* sat. Even though Larisa and Anatolii had never been alone together, their engagement had not gone unsuspected by the church grandmothers. "Larisa and Anatolii will walk together," the pastor said with a smile. "The wedding will be held Sunday, June 15, after our worship time."

In Russia, Christian weddings and communist weddings are markedly different. Communist weddings are held in wedding palaces—state buildings where as many as fifty couples a day are married in quick procession.

At the wedding palace each couple, with their friends and relatives, is ushered into an ornate room. One or two officials—frequently women—preside over the ten-minute ceremony in which they urge the couple to "work faithfully for the sake of the beloved motherland and rear children who will be ardent patriots and builders of communism."

The newlyweds sign documents, receive new internal passports to show their changed marital status, and then are pronounced man and wife. After a quick glass of champagne, they move along to make room for the next couple.

Often the newlyweds proceed straight from the palace to place their wedding bouquet on a monument honoring Lenin or World War II heroes. If they are fortunate enough to own a car or borrow one for the day, they deck it with streams of balloons and attach a doll to the front grille for good luck.

Christian weddings in Russia are joyously welcomed as an opportunity for a legitimate mass evangelistic meeting. From the first day of their engagement, Larisa and Anatolii started to plan and pray that their wedding would be a witness for Christ.

The couple wrote their wedding invitations on post-cards. Larisa decorated each postcard with a flower border. In a festive script Anatolii copied Psalm 34: 3 in the center of each postcard: "O magnify the Lord with me, and let us exalt his name together."

The whole church helped with the preparations. They decided to hold the wedding at the home of the Orlovs*, since they had removed some walls from their house in order to hold meetings. The forest bordered the Orlovs' backyard—a pleasant setting that would also help make the wedding more secluded.

Counting everyone from the church, Christians from other towns, and non-Christian neighbors, Larisa and Anatolii expected at least three hundred guests—more than both their families together could provide food for. But the young couple, who were accustomed to thinking of the whole church as one family, knew that the members would help provide the traditional wedding dinner.

Preparations for Anatolii and Larisa's wedding progressed smoothly until two days before the ceremony. That day twenty young people and Iosif D., a deacon, arrived in Barnaul after traveling a hundred miles from the city of M. They had come to sing in the wedding choir and play in the orchestra.

The choir gathered that afternoon for a rehearsal at the Orlovs' house. During the sermon—invariably a part of a Christian choir rehearsal in Russia—Iosif preached on Judas's betrayal of Jesus. During the service, a woman from Barnaul who had asked to join the wedding choir slipped quietly from the meeting.

Thirty minutes later the police had surrounded the house. They demanded that Iosif come with them to the police station.

*pseudonym

97

"I don't think I ought to be going with you," he replied. "I have come all the way from M. for this wedding—that's why I'm wearing this suit."

By this time Larisa, Anatolii, and the other young people in the choir were on their knees praying loudly, pleading with God to deliver Iosif. Their prayers frightened the police. They bound Iosif's wrists and pulled him to the black wagon parked by the door.

"But I'm not charged with any offense," Iosif protested. "I'm a free man, not a criminal!"

Inside the wagon, the police accused, "You say you are Iosif—you are really Vania, the traveling evangelist. At last we have caught up with you!"

"But my passport—" Iosif pleaded. "You can clearly see my name—I am Iosif, not Vania."

"Falsified!" the policeman, who was also a KGB interrogator, snorted. "And you pretend you have come for a wedding!" He turned toward Iosif in the back seat of the black wagon. "Do not think you are deceiving us. We know your weddings—just another excuse for your fanatical meetings. It's another trick to pull Soviet citizens into your church. Real Soviet citizens are married in wedding palaces!"

Strangely, the police parked the black wagon several blocks from the police station. "We'll walk the rest of the way," the KGB interrogator ordered, unlocking the back door.

Iosif noticed a public washroom across the street. He asked for permission to step inside.

"I simply don't understand to this day how it all happened," Iosif recalls. "When I spoke to him, the guard simply nodded and turned his back. Inside the washroom, I heard a great commotion. My guard was shouting to the KGB interrogator that I had suddenly disap-

The Barnaul youth group circa 1958. (When the government's local watchdog for religious groups learned of this photo, he demanded a copy and the names of those pictured.)

The frame house on Radishchevskaia Street which the Barnaul congregation bought in the 1940s to use for their meetings (below). It served as their place of worship until January, 1961, when local authorities padlocked it. (The address was later changed from 49 to 67 due to new construction on the street.)

A hand-written hymnal.

A mound of dirt remains at 22 Strelochnaia Street, site of the large brick house purchased by the Evald Gaufs and Yekaterina Shirobokova for a meeting place. The house was bulldozed on March 17, 1966, because it would "corrupt students at the nearby school."

Nikolai Kuzmich Khmara
in his coffin following his
1964 torture and martyrdom.
His widow and children
are in the front row.

The iron fence
around Khmara's grave
did not prevent vandals
from removing his monument
less than a month
after it was erected.

Siberian Christians lead Khmara's funeral procession with a wreathed inscription, "For to me to live is Christ, and to die is gain." Elderly believers ride in the vehicle behind the hearse; others walk alongside.

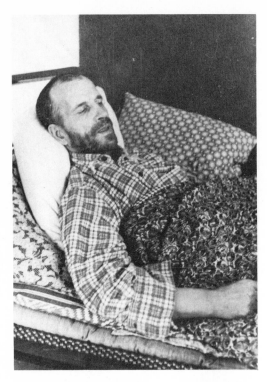

When sentenced for a third time in November, 1971, presbyter Miniakov began a hunger strike, which effected an early release. In this photo he recuperates in the home of fellow believers.

Eager Christians wait outside the Barnaul prison for the 1970 release
of presbyter Dmitrii Vasilevich Miniakov, shown (left) with his wife
Antonina and their two youngest sons.

Yurii Mikhalkov, Komsomol
member, college graduate,
and respected engineer,
became a believer at age 25.
Eight months later he was
arrested for organizing
a "harmful" religious meeting.
After two years in jail,
he was exonerated—and
given a job sweeping streets
near his alma mater.

peared. I saw the other police scatter and start to search through the crowd. At any moment, I expected them to burst into the washroom, but surprisingly they did not enter the building.

"When the police had moved on and the search subsided, I simply walked outside and up the street. I saw that swarms of reinforcements had been called from the station and had surrounded the whole area ahead and set up a barricade. People were being searched. I stepped back, watched from a distance, and noticed that the police were allowing buses and automobiles to go through unsearched. I walked back to the bus stop, shoved in among the crowd pushing onto the bus, and the police waved our vehicle through the barricade.

"I returned to the choir rehearsal that had become a prayer meeting. 'I told you I would return if it was God's will,' I said, and embraced the tearful young people."

Anatolii and Larisa's wedding day dawned sunny. Only the dread of the almost certain return of the police hung over the happy day.

By ten that morning almost three hundred people had gathered for the worship service and wedding at the Orlovs' house. Larisa and Anatolii had strung a wedding banner across the front wall: THOU WILT SHOW ME THE PATH OF LIFE.

For the first and last time, the bride and bridegroom sat together in the front of the congregation during the worship service. By the next Sunday Larisa would sit on the women's side of the church and Anatolii with the men. Larisa wore a long white dress, and in her hair she braided a garland of *fialki* (violets). Anatolii had tucked a fern in his jacket lapel. Solemnly the young couple listened.

Pastor Grigorii preached the first sermon. "Even as we

99

have in our meeting today a bride and bridegroom, Christ the bridegroom is one day coming for his Bride the Church. Are you ready to meet him?"

Iosif, the deacon from M., preached on the purpose of Christian marriage. Soberly he reminded the congregation, "The words of the apostle Paul are for our church today. 'The time is short: it remaineth, that both they that have wives be as though they had none' (I Cor. 7:29). Our first allegiance—married or unmarried—is to the Lord." For the next thirty minutes Iosif spoke practically about God's will for single persons. "Christ has a purpose and place for every member of his body," he emphasized.

After the sermons and the singing, Pastor Grigorii beckoned Antolii and Larisa to the front. With the congregation as their witness, he asked the young people the customary questions. "Are you marrying of your own free will? Will you live together according to the will of God? Will you be faithful to each other to the end? Will you establish a Christian home and raise your children to follow Christ? Are you willing to endure persecution for the Gospel?"

After the vows, Larisa and Anatolii each prayed aloud. Then the parents of the bride and bridegroom prayed. Other members of the church also prayed at length for the young couple.

Grigorii prayed last. Then he placed Larisa's hand in Anatolii's. "The life verse I give to you," he announced soberly, "is Matthew 6:33, 'But seek ye first the kingdom of God, and his righteousness; and all these things shall be added unto you.' " Slowly the choir sang:

> In the presence of God's people
> These two hands and lives are joined
> To walk a barren way with love,
> To labor for the good of man,

To hold each other closely through
The joys and sorrows of their lives.
May thy tender hand, O Father,
Guide them on their earthly way.

In thy presence, heavenly Word,
Their lips have spoken vows;
To thee they pledge their faithfulness
To one another until death.
As they daily live before thee,
May their vows more precious grow,
Nurtured by a Word eternal
To fulfill the will of God.

As two names are joined together
To unite them into one,
In this unity, through storm
And sickness, trouble, pain, and joy,
Preserve them, God all-righteous, as
They live the oneness thou hast blessed,
And may thy name of endless praise
Become a song for all their days.

The following celebration lasted all afternoon and evening and into the next day. Dahlias, violets, gladioli, and ferns decked the house. *Babushki* from the church baked the wedding dinner—steaming *borsch,* potatoes, fruit *kompot,* and fresh *bulochki* (buns). There were songs, poems, and even some humorous stories.

That evening Larisa and Anatolii opened their gifts— the most important, a scrapbook containing a complete record of their wedding day that had been meticulously written by hand that morning. All their lives they could reread the hymns that had been sung. The words of the sermon would be in the scrapbook to guide and comfort them during the years ahead.

Before the long day was over, more than 350 people had participated in the wedding celebration. Twenty people had preached short sermons. At least forty non-believers attended—a cause for great gladness to the believers who otherwise had so little opportunity to share the Gospel with these non-Christian friends.

Larisa's mother had invited Marina I., a neighbor from the apartment across the hall, to her daughter's wedding. Marina had never attended a Christian wedding before. When she left the Orlovs' house that evening, she embraced Larisa's mother and thanked her warmly for the invitation. "You *veruiushchie* . . . " she mumbled, "I just cannot understand—your weddings are so peaceful and orderly. Just last week I attended the wedding of my nephew. Vodka was flowing, dishes were flying, . . ."

It was 2:00 A.M. by the time the last guests told the newlyweds good-bye. An hour and a half later Larisa and Anatolii rode the trolley car to Larisa's parents' apartment, where they would live until they were fortunate enough to find an apartment of their own. Larisa and Anatolii had both taken their three-day wedding leave of absence from their factories before the ceremony so that they could help prepare for the celebration. In a few hours they would both return to work.

For both of them, their wedding had been the most glorious day of their lives. The sermons . . . the songs . . . the love of the church family.

And the police had not returned.

8

The Martyrdom

ALMOST EVERYONE IN KULUNDA, a town of fourteen thousand about two hundred miles southwest of Barnaul, knew about Nikolai Kuzmich Khmara's drunken carousings.

Despite his reputation for being able to drink as much vodka as any man in town, Khmara was active in a communist club and considered one of Kulunda's most influential citizens.

People affectionately called him a *prostoi chelovek*–a simple, true Russian person. "You can depend on Nikolai Kuzmich," his comrades often said. Sober or drunk, Khmara seemed the same—equally ready to laugh or to play melancholy songs on his *baian* (accordion).

Through the witness of Feoktist Ivanovich Subbotin, a presbyter from an unregistered Kulunda church, Nikolai's brother Vasilii and his wife were converted to Christ. The seemingly carefree Nikolai was profoundly impressed by the change in his brother and sister-in-law. When he noticed the peace that pervaded their lives, his own lack of purpose began to haunt him. In the summer of 1963, 34-year-old Nikolai and his wife Mariia Ivanovna came to Christ and joined the unregistered group of believers meeting in Kulunda.

Nikolai Khmara never did things halfway. When he became a believer, he told the other Christians, "If I'm going to be a *veruiushchii,* I'm going to live completely for Jesus Christ. I'm not holding back anything."

He meant what he said. Soon all of Kulunda was whispering about Nikolai's remarkable transformation. He had seemed to be such a devoted communist, a staunch product of the system.

Now Nikolai fervently shared his faith. He often sang the hymn, "I Am Called to Work in the World":

> Stand against all idols,
> Fear not faithless friends,
> Witness to the world,
> Regarding not its judgment.

In a sermon he preached to the Kulunda congregation that fall, Nikolai said, "If a person lives for Jesus Christ, he should be ready for anything and must be true to Christ to the end."

Nikolai was to experience the reality of those words with shocking suddenness.

During the Christmas holidays—December 24-27, 1963—Nikolai, his brother Vasilii, sister-in-law Liubov, and the presbyter Subbotin were called before the court in Kulunda.

A Soviet legal publication, *Sovetskaia Yustitsiia,* later described the government's version of the accusations against the four Christians and revealed that in reality they were punished solely for their Christian activities—particularly their bold participation in Kulunda's unregistered church:

Feoktist Ivanovich Subbotin, Liubov Mikhailovna Khmara, and the brothers Nikolai Kuzmich and Vasilii Kuzmich Khmara were brought before the court. The court proceedings lasted four days. For four days the judges of the Altai regional court painstakingly investigated the activities of the Kulunda sect.

The accused pleaded not guilty, announcing that they had committed no crime whatsoever. Then they refused to give evidence on the substance of the accusation.

They carefully concealed from the court the contents of sermons preached at their services. However, as a result of the witnesses' testimony and evidence collected during the investigation, the accused were convicted of bringing up minors in isolation from social life by drawing them into their group; of urging believers to reject their responsibilities as citizens; of inciting citizens to disobey the auxiliary police; of refusing to join trade unions; and in general avoiding all forms of social activity.

They held illegal prayer meetings at night, in unsanitary conditions and with minors present. The senior sanitary inspector of the Kulunda district stated that the building in which the prayer meetings had taken place was unsuitable for the religious services held by this congregation, according to the accepted standards of sanitation and hygiene. (The cubic capacity of air was insufficient and there was no ventilation.)

An unregistered community of Evangelical Christians and Baptists has existed in Kulunda for a long time. This community had preached the Bible and observed the religious practices laid down by the AUCECB. Since 1961, all kinds of addresses, notices, and other texts criticizing the AUCECB appeared among the Baptists. From this time the activities of some of the community's members have taken on a reactionary character.

In 1962 the chairman of the Kulunda Settlement Soviet demanded that the community either be registered or cease holding meetings.

The older members obeyed, but the younger ones, with Subbotin at their head, broke away. They began holding illegal meetings at night. This section of the Baptists refused to recognize the official AUCECB statutes and evaded the control of the laws on religious cults enforced in the Soviet Union.

Subbotin organized an illegal school for training young Baptists. After the course, examinations were held during which the youth were given cards with such questions as: "On which day did God create the world? On which day did God create man?" Yet the day on which Subbotin began to harm the state, our society, and citizens (including believers themselves) was of no interest to him.

The criminal court of the Altai Region sentenced Subbotin, the organizer of the reactionary Kulunda Baptists, to five years' imprisonment; the brothers Nikolai and Vasilii Khmara to three years; and gave Liubov Khmara a conditional sentence because of extenuating circumstances.[1]

For the Christians' version of what happened, it is necessary to turn to a document dated February 16, 1964, and signed by 120 Christians from Barnaul and Kulunda.

It was December 24-27, 1963, that Nikolai Khmara, with Brother Feoktist Ivanovich Subbotin and Khmara's brother and sister-in-law, Vasilii Kuzmich Khmara and Liubov Mikhailovna Khmara, appeared before the court and together with others was sentenced for the name of Christ . . . and for acting according to conscience.

Beloved brothers and sisters, we know that the first question that will arise in your mind is—why? What official charges were brought against Khmara by the court of prosecutors? . . . .

In reply, we present some excerpts from the sentence rendered by the Altai regional court, case number 142, where it is stated that "a group of Baptists conducted illegal meetings under unsanitary conditions, drawing the youth into a sectarian group. Under cover of 'purifying,' the sectarians conducted propaganda against the AUCECB and its statutes and maintained contact with other similar illegal groups." Other similar allegations were directed against the Baptists.

In the closing accusations it is stated that the guilt of the accused is supported by the following evidence: "Regarding reactionary activity harmful to society, certain people declared that the group of sectarians headed by F. I. Subbotin and his active supporters, N. K. Khmara, V. K. Khmara, and L. M. Khmara, analyzed various biblical texts, permitted independent and incorrect interpretations, criticized and did not accept the new constitution of the AUCECB."

There you have all the evidence of reactionary activity harmful to society. One might think that the witnesses were members of the Holy Synod, people with higher theological education, well-versed in biblical truths, and called to defend their purity. Not at all!

Dear brothers and sisters: the fact is that the world cannot be permitted the illegally acquired right to interpret the Bible to us by atheistic standards. The world has no right to send to our churches their "servants" . . . and to do away with all servants who are called by the Lord and elected by the church. . . .

Perhaps those who appeared before the court really were criminals? Not at all. They are no more guilty than any of us who believe in the Lord Jesus Christ. Their entire guilt lies in the fact that they did not hesitate to hold meetings, to allow youth to attend them, to have contact with other congregations, and to speak out against the AUCECB and its constitution.

Some may think the judges were exceptional. No, the judges themselves were quite ordinary, modern judges. They're the same as those who are conducting similar "courts of justice" and condemning plainly innocent believers.

By this letter we do not want to create in you a feeling of hatred toward our persecutors. Even though this evil is done by wicked people, they did not do it on their own. They have been led and encouraged to do evil.

No less guilty of this murder are those who unceasingly publish lies in the papers on the basis of which court proceedings are begun and wild hatred is stirred up against believers. This is a collective sin of our world.

Let us look upon our persecutors as Christ has taught us: "But I say unto you, Love your enemies, bless them that curse you, do good to them that hate you, and pray for them which despitefully use you, and persecute you" (Matthew 5:44).

Our Lord says: "Rejoice, and be exceeding glad: for great is your reward in heaven. . ." (Matthew 5:12). We are being condemned not for evil works, nor for breaking laws, but for good deeds—for not recognizing the AUCECB and its constitution which causes the church to decay but which is so profitable to the judges for condemning believers that they continue to sentence on the basis of that constitution even after the constitution has been rejected. . . .

On January 11, two weeks after sentencing, Nikolai's wife Mariia Ivanovna received a telegram from the Barnaul Investigatory Prison of the First Altai Administration for the Preservation of Public Order. Her husband was dead. Her four children, ages one month to thirteen years, were fatherless. The prison told her to come for her husband's body.

On January 13, the widow and relatives of the dead man, together with Christians from Barnaul and Kulunda, received the body of Nikolai Khmara from the prison.

The Christians wrote sadly:

. . . Not only have the betrayers of the truth and the church caused many tears and much suffering to the children of God, but continuing their shameful activity and sin against God have added to their iniquity the death of our dear brother, Nikolai Kuzmich Khmara.

Yes, in our day a deed has taken place "which has not been done nor seen." Heed what has happened. Tell this to everyone great and small so that all who fear God and long to meet Christ may in one Spirit turn to him, defend, and hold fast to the truth.

"And now, Lord, behold their threatenings: and grant unto thy servants, that with all boldness they may speak thy word" (Acts 4: 29).

During the trial, Nikolai had been in robust health and cheerful. But when the Christians opened the casket, they found the tortured body of an old man. Chain marks scarred his hands. Burns scorched the palms of his hands and soles of his feet. The nails had been torn from his fingers and toes. A sharp, red-hot object had left gaping wounds in his abdomen. Both feet showed signs of puncture wounds, and the body was swollen and bruised.

Khmara's mouth was stuffed with cotton. Yevgenii K., one of the Barnaul deacons, stood by the coffin when the cotton was removed. He recalls, "Nikolai Kuzmich's tongue had been torn out. Later we heard from other prisoners that our brother had spent his final breath telling the guards about Jesus. The authorities could not stop Khmara's testimony. But they tore out his tongue to stop him from talking about Christ."

Later Mariia Khmara learned from another Christian, held in the same prison, that her husband had suffered psychological as well as physical torture in the terrible days after the trial. The Christian said that Khmara had been given injections to try to change his personality.

In the document entitled "Cry from Siberia," the 120 Christians from Kulunda and Barnaul told their story to "all the children of God who compose the Church of Jesus Christ—to all Evangelical Christians-Baptists living in our land, from east to west and from north to south."

When we saw all this, we had mixed feelings—of deep grief and joy. We grieve that our dear brother Nikolai Kuzmich had to pass through such brutal trials and accept death in the prison walls. We grieve for the unhealed wounds made by godless hands upon the innocent hearts of children—not for evil deeds, but for good—for love to the people, to the Lord, and for his name. Nikolai Kuzmich bore it all as a good soldier of Jesus Christ and was faithful to him unto death. We are filled with deep sorrow at seeing the widow and children crying at the casket, hardly recognizing the face of their father. Yet we comforted them and were ourselves comforted with the fact that we all have the Father of orphans and widows, and there is a righteous Judge—Christ.

The Christians wrote in another document, "No one says that this bestial murder was done on instructions from Moscow. It was a result of the intolerance of the local authorities, who, however, always follow whatever trend the central authorities have ordained in connection with Christian believers."

The authorities had hoped Khmara's tortured body would intimidate Christians in Kulunda and Barnaul. Khmara's murder, they surmised, would serve as a warning to the bold Christians from the two areas. But in fact, Khmara's martyrdom only made the government's injustice more searing to the Christians. They determined to appeal to Soviet authorities for an honest investigation.

The Christians sent photos of Khmara's tortured body and a detailed account of the trial and murder to local authorities and also to officials in Moscow. They asked that a commission be sent to investigate the crime and see Khmara's tortured body themselves.

The Christians waited by Khmara's casket for the commission to arrive. They solemnly conducted several Gospel services. Meanwhile, the KGB, the Altai Territorial Procurator's office, and the Territorial Executive Committee terrorized the mourners at Dmitrii Miniakov's house in which Khmara's body lay, summoning them to their jobs with threats of all possible penalties.

But the official commission did not come. Undeterred, the Christians determined that the world should hear Khmara's story. Tenaciously, they guarded the records and films of Khmara's trial and torture and at one point even buried some film so it could not be confiscated by the police. They took additional photos—knowing they must have evidence if the official commission ever did arrive.

Then the believers prepared for the funeral to be held on January 16 in Barnaul. Barnaul officials had hoped Khmara would be buried with as little public display as possible—with decorum the officials considered befitting to a communist society.

In the Soviet Union, decorous communist funerals are carried out with dispatch. In a typical Russian city like Barnaul, forty rubles ($53) procures a thirty-minute funeral. Mourners enter a stark room where funeral music is piped over a loudspeaker (sometimes at an extra cost of five rubles). Customarily, several of the mourners stand on chairs and deliver eulogies to the deceased— often accompanied by unconsoled weeping from families whose Marxist upbringing has taught them that there is no hope of life after death.

At the end of thirty minutes, the papier-mache coffin, bedecked with any medals or awards the deceased has received, exits by a conveyor belt, and an attendant ushers the mourners out of the room. Nonreligious families most frequently choose cremation, which is less expensive.

Traditionally, communist officials do not interfere with funerals, even Christian ones. Knowing this, the believers meticulously planned Khmara's burial.

The day of the funeral the believers first held a two-hour evangelistic meeting at the house of Dmitrii Miniakov, who was still in prison. Konstantin, one of the Barnaul preachers, recalls, "Khmara's death reached more people than twenty preachers."

The Christians had carefully constructed a wooden casket and tucked flowers and fir boughs around Khmara's body, which they had dressed in a black suit and white shirt (see photo section). The morning of the funeral, KGB officials sent a hearse, demanding that the Christians use it to transport the casket to the graveyard. But the Christians refused to conceal the body. They carried the open casket through the city themselves. Only after they had reached the outskirts of the city did they consent to use the hearse.

The Christians prepared large placards with Bible quotations for the funeral procession:

"For to me to live is Christ, and to die is gain" (Philippians 1: 21).

"Fear not them which kill the body . . . but rather fear him which is able to destroy both soul and body in hell" (Matthew 10: 28).

"I saw under the altar the souls of them that were slain

112

for the word of God" (Revelation 6:9).

With the casket on the shoulders of pallbearers and Scripture placards scattered throughout the hundreds of people who had gathered, the crowd plodded through wintery Barnaul to the graveyard. Several times they paused along the way to preach and read Scriptures.

The Christians had planned to march through the center of town, but permission was denied, and they had to route their procession along the edge of the city. Nevertheless, they sang as they filed through the snowy streets, attracting much attention:

Home of wonder! prepared in heaven
For those who loved their Lord in this life.
From the sorrows of earth, I am bound for glory
With joys eternal awaiting me there.

Home of wonder! where angels sing
And all creation answering
Forever praises Christ the Lamb,
The King all worthy of honor and power.

Home of wonder! in heavenly glory
We shall see Christ in splendor and joy.
In the garden of God in that verdant land
We shall see what no eye has yet seen.

Home of wonder! so soon we shall see it.
And greet those we loved who were dear to us here.
Then our Savior will dry our tears with his love
And receive us eternally into his peace.

At the graveside the Christians conducted another evangelistic service, rejoicing that their brother's soul was with God. Then they lowered Khmara's body into the grave that men from the church had dug, and hammered a simple wooden cross over it.

During the burial and for several days afterward, police guarded the grave to make sure Khmara's body stayed safely buried and that the Christians did not transport the battered corpse elsewhere as evidence of Soviet brutality.

In April, the Irkutsk KGB entered a political criminal case against a Christian from Prokopevsk, a town 130 miles northeast of Barnaul. P. F. Zakharov was convicted for "slandering Soviet authorities" because he had circulated the Khmara story and was sentenced to three years of strict discipline and hard labor.

Eight years later, in April, 1972, on a Russian Orthodox memorial day that follows Easter, the evangelical Christians decided to hold a commemorative service at Khmara's grave. The young people recounted Khmara's story. The choir sang, the orchestra played, and the preachers spoke powerfully. From all over the cemetery people who had come for the memorial day gathered to listen to the message of hope preached by the believers who, humanly speaking, might have lost reason for hope long ago.

The night before the memorial service, the Christians had placed a tombstone at Khmara's grave. Together they had decided on the inscription:

NIKOLAI KUZMICH KHMARA
BORN 1916
MARTYRED 1964
TORTURED TO DEATH BECAUSE
HE PROCLAIMED JESUS CHRIST
—CHRISTIANS IN RUSSIA

The Christians had asked a stonecutter to inscribe the tombstone. Fearfully, he turned them away. "If the authorities found out that I did this for you, it would be prison for me!" he said. So they inscribed the tombstone themselves and placed Khmara's photo beside the inscription.

Although it was protected by an iron fence, the monument was torn down later that month by unknown persons who used an acetylene torch to sever it.

Khmara's relatives complained to the regional procurator of the Barnaul region about the desecration of the monument. They also sent a telegram to Moscow protesting, "You don't even leave the dead in peace!" They were told that the procurator removed the tombstone to use as evidence for a criminal case of "slander against Soviet reality."

But despite years of struggle by the Soviet government to stifle Khmara's story, the news of his death spread across Russia. Christians were shocked and saddened but strengthened in their faith. A poet from one of the churches wrote:

And now blood flows again.
Siberia is a second Coliseum,
Dogs devour Odintsov,
The order is given, "Finish them off!"
Others have been tortured,
And that has happened elsewhere
Than in Kulunda, which witnessed recent murder—
Our dearest Brother Khmara sad struck down. . . .
Formerly they used to raise a church
Where the remains of martyrs lay interred.
What now have persecutions given us?
They bear new life to churches everywhere.[2]

1. *Sovetskaya Yustitsia*, September, 1964, p. 27.
2. Quoted by Michael Bourdeaux, in *Faith on Trial in Russia*, Hodder and Stoughton, London, 1971, p. 97.

9

Songs of Deliverance

FEBRUARY, 1964, THE MONTH AFTER Khmara's death, was a bitter, biting month in Barnaul. Children bundled in snowsuits, scarves and *valenki* (little felt boots) waddled beside *babushki* who dutifully brought their grandchildren outdoors for fresh air even in freezing weather. Men wearing wool caps with wide ear flaps, two pairs of gloves, two jackets, and rough, thick cotton pants pulled sleds with food supplies at a run so that they and their groceries wouldn't freeze before reaching their own door. Grandfathers joked, "Barnaul has one season—twelve months of winter."

On one of those freezing nights, February 29—a month and a half after Khmara's death—Christians from the unregistered congregation in Barnaul gathered for a meeting at the home of Aleksandr Gushchin.

Many times they had met without disruption by the police. But the raids came frequently enough that the Christians were not particularly surprised when five swearing, shouting *druzhinniki* and their *militsiia* leader shoved into the Gushchins' tiny house that night.

Some of the *druzhinniki* were drunk. All were disgrun-

116

tled at being forced to come out into the icy Siberian night to track down Christians. They had come in a large truck—too large to drive onto the small access road near the Gushchin home. Consequently, they had to park half a kilometer away and tramp through swirling snow that threatened to turn into a blizzard.

A hundred fifty Christians had crowded into the house. Most had managed to sit on narrow benches brought in especially for the meeting. But the benches were lined so closely that the knees of the people in one row nudged the backs of the people in front of them.

The *druzhinniki* demanded that the "mob" disperse. The believers instinctively moved even closer together. They formed a barricade between the police and the pastors at the front of the room, continuing to sing loudly.

The police were not in the mood for negotiations. They were angry and anxious to finish their assignment. When they saw they could not break through the congregation to the pastors, they started to pull the people closest to the door outside into the hall.

They also phoned the police station for reinforcements. Fifteen more *druzhinniki* were deployed with the order, "Be bolder and more energetic. You won't suffer for it."

The police dragged some believers out the door by their arms and legs. The *druzhinniki* pulled Nadia L., five months pregnant, out the door by her heavy braid wound tightly around her head. Nadia pled for permission to at least be allowed to take her coat. In reply, one of the *druzhinniki* shoved her out into the night. "You are coming with us now!" he snarled.

Nadia recalls, "I thought of the words from the Bible, 'Agree with thine adversary quickly, while thou art in the

117

way with him; lest at any time the adversary deliver thee to the judge, and the judge deliver thee to the officer, and thou be cast into prison.' After all, what can you do when several men grab you and start dragging you through the door?"

The *druzhinniki* thrust Nadia and three others onto the truck. The Christians huddled together for warmth—frightened of the danger of frostbite. Then, although paralyzed from cold, they started to sing. "The whistling wind was our accompaniment," Nadia remembers.

Only a few more days
Are left for us to walk
The narrow, thorn-hedged roads,
Bearing the burden of Christ.

While our strength remains,
If he commands that we
Shall labor, then with courage
We'll bear the cross he gives.

Only a few more days
Are left for us to work
Before we're sheltered from pain
And at home in his glorious light.

Back at the Gushchins' house, the *militsiia* leader had decided to take several more people to the police station, hoping that this would end the meeting and perhaps finally teach the stubborn Christians a lesson.

However, when the pastors at the front of the packed room saw what was happening, they shouted to the police, "Wait! If you are going to take some of us—then you must take us all. Just give us a minute to put on our coats and we will come!"

"We're one family," another pastor announced loudly

118

to the police. But the congregation knew his words were also meant to encourage them. "We will stand together. What happens to one will happen to all."

Uncertain whether taking all the Christians meant a coup or chaos, the police hesitated. But the Christians had swiftly pulled on their coats and were surging toward the captors.

Nadia and the three other Christians crouched in a corner of the truck, expecting the vehicle to leave for the police station at any moment. Nadia could not help thinking how comforting it would be if her husband Lev were beside her. *But the nine children at home,* Nadia thought sensibly. *If anything happens to me, Lev will have to care for them.*

Then she saw what looked like a dark cloud coming through the blizzard. Over the howling wind she heard singing. "You can't imagine my joy when I saw the other Christians coming," Nadia recalls, "It was our brothers and sisters—our family joining us to help us in our time of need."

Curious neighbors creaked open their double windows to peer into the stormy night at the strange scene by the truck—people embracing, singing, praying. Police shouted, swore, and shoved.

But when the whole group had gathered by the truck, the *druzhinniki* faced a problem. One hundred fifty Christians, plus police reinforcements, would not fit into the truck. Furiously, they herded their prisoners into the snow-swept street for the long march to the station. But the police, wrapped in long overcoats and *dushegreiki*— sheepskin vests called "soul-warmers"—were not suffering from the cold.

The four Christians who had come without their coats were freezing. The others quickly shared their wraps. "I can still see Yurii with Zoia's kerchief tied tightly under his chin," Nadia remembers with a laugh. "But we didn't care if we looked like clowns. We were so glad for any warmth to protect us against the blizzard."

Arm in arm the Christians marched away from the truck singing:

> If we place our trust in Jesus,
> Light will shine upon our way,
> Joy will fill our hearts each day,
> No discouragement will stay.

"As we marched, we made such a strange procession that people could not help noticing us through the blizzard," Nadia recalls. "We did not want to miss an opportunity to testify to them about Christ. The authorities would never have given us permission to preach on the street, but they could hardly prevent prisoners from singing. We even felt a happiness, because we were suffering for the sake of Christ. We remembered that Christ sang as he left the Last Supper for the Garden of Gethsemane."

The leader of the foray against the Christians phoned ahead to the police station. He requested that trucks and more police be sent to transport the Christians.

Druzhinniki reinforcements had gathered at the Communist Club of the Eastern Village, where a film was being shown. They waited in the lobby to keep warm. As the 150 Christians appeared outside the club, the movie finished. The *druzhinniki* poured into the street, but so did the crowd from the cinema.

The curious citizens intermingled with the Christians. "What have you done?" they asked. "Where are they taking you? Really? Because you are a *veruiushchii?*"

By now the blizzard was blowing wildly. In the confusion of the crowd, the police searched frantically for their prisoners. "All Christians to the left—non-Christians to the right!" the *militsiia* leader bellowed into the blizzard. "No mixing!"

When the police had finally succeeded in separating the crowd, they herded the Christians into the two covered trucks that had been summoned from the police station.

The police pushed the Christians like cattle onto the trucks—hollering, hitting, and in some cases hurting their prisoners. The blizzard blew so bitterly that people could not recognize each other. The stormy night had turned into a surrealistic nightmare.

The crowd from the cinema did not disperse. They gaped as the police herded the harmless Christians onto the trucks. Some crossed to the Christians' side of the street in protest. Even some of the police started to grumble about such a "crude assignment."

Inside the covered vans the Christians trembled from cold and fear. Their greatest worry was that the two trucks would drive to separate destinations. "As long as we were together, we felt we could face our suffering," Nadia remembers. To keep their courage in Christ from faltering, they started to sing.

To their great relief, both trucks arrived at the October Region Executive Committee building. With renewed courage the prisoners marched into the government building singing the hymn "Joy of Salvation."

Joy of salvation
We sing today,
All our thanksgiving
Bring to the Lord.

121

Heaven and earth
With joy praise his name.
Miracle-working
Name we proclaim.

His precious blood,
Has saved us from sin.
By his stripes we are healed,
By his loss we are found.

The power of death
He broke in his death.
He bore our blame
And canceled the curse.

With praise in our hearts
We'll gratefully raise
Our songs throughout life
And forever in heaven.

Nadia remembers the remarkable triumphant entry of
the prisoners. "As our 150-voice choir sang, the songs
echoed through the high halls of the Communist Party
building as if it were a cathedral. There must have been
about five hundred police altogether surrounding us
inside the building. What an opportunity we had to testify through our singing!"

"What are you trying to do—hold a Gospel service in
this building?" one of the *militsiia* leaders growled. The
Christians sang all the louder, and the police met in
another room to discuss the fate of their prisoners.

About nine-thirty that night the Christians were released, but Yakov Bil, Aleksandr Gushchin, and Vladimir Firsov were each fined fifty rubles. One of the
druzhinniki who took part in disrupting the prayer meeting later said, "We shouldn't just disperse sectarians—
they should be strangled or imprisoned. . . ." The head of

the area KGB, Comrade I. F. Petrov, defended this statement vigorously.

Outside the police station, the Christians gathered in an empty yard to pray and praise God for delivering them from the hands of the police. Afterwards, they walked arm in arm to the nearby apartment of a Christian—and with great thanksgiving to God continued their meeting.

10

Appeal to the Kremlin

IT WAS IN 1964 that an official delegate dispatched by the government from Moscow visited the unregistered Barnaul congregation and urged them to return to the registered church at 67 Radishchevskaia Street. Some of the other Christians had already done so when the authorities reopened the building in 1962. However, the delegate warned them not to bring their children nor to pray openly for prisoners.

Many unregistered congregations like the one in Barnaul considered such restrictions intolerable. By 1964 these unregistered congregations were gaining strength all over Russia. As early as 1960, unregistered congregations had begun to weld into a national fellowship, and presbyter Dmitrii Miniakov was a member of the organizing council of unregistered churches.

Because they took the initiative to call for a congress of the AUCECB that fully represented all Baptists in the Soviet Union, these unregistered reformers were first known as the *Initsiativnaia Gruppa* (or *Initsiativniki*). At this point the *Initsiativniki* still held hope of bringing about reforms which they felt were needed from within the church.

Partially because of the prodding of the *Initsiativniki*, the AUCECB received permission from the government to hold a congress in 1963, after almost twenty years of not being allowed to convene. Seemingly in response to the appeals of the reformers, the congress significantly eased parts of the New Statutes and Letter of Instructions.* The AUCECB made some other overtures toward reconciliation with the *Initsiativniki*. However, the reformers were not allowed genuine representation at the congress. In fact, 150 of the most prominent reformers were already in prison by 1963.[1]

Among the prisoners were the five Barnaul believers (including presbyter Dmitrii Miniakov and engineer Yurii Mikhalkov) who had been tried in May of that year (chapter 5). Some of the men had been sentenced to strict regime. Among other restrictions, strict regime meant heavier work loads and lower food rations. One prisoner on strict regime recalls, "Several barracks away from the kitchen, we could smell the rotten fish and potatoes cooking. At dinner we were served only small portions of these. For breakfast and supper we were allotted six spoons of porridge."

Christians in the congregation at Barnaul suffered with their imprisoned brothers. One of the deacons explains, "Our entire church was so grieved for our brethren that we felt our hearts would break. During this time I had terrible headaches and couldn't sleep. I could not help thinking of our dear brothers lying on wooden benches in the Barnaul prison. As I ate my supper, I wondered if my brothers even had food. How could we

---

*At the next AUCECB congress in 1966, the New Statutes and Letter of Instructions were largely repealed and a new constitution was adopted. Thus, the pressure for reform exerted by the CCECB benefited both registered and unregistered churches.

who were free relax when we knew our brothers were suffering?

"I knew that government provocateurs are often purposely placed in prisoners' cells to spy and try to force other prisoners to turn against Christians. And our brothers were not permitted to see and encourage each other inside the prison.

"The greatest hardship was that our brothers were not allowed to have Bibles. Almost every day, they were searched. The guards look harder for Scripture than they do for knives or weapons. But our brothers did have some Scriptures among them that God miraculously protected!"

In 1964, relatives of Christian prisoners boldly banded together to form a Council of Prisoners' Relatives (CPR). A report from the First All-Union Conference of Prisoners' Relatives confirmed that the fears of the Barnaul Christians were not unfounded:

> The condition of those in prisons and camps is horrible. For praying at bedside and for witnessing about Christ, prisoners face solitary confinement and are deprived of food parcels and family visits. They may not send letters with religious verses back and forth to relatives. Prisoners can neither possess nor read the Bible. They are subject to all kinds of repression and constant interrogations, but they may go free if they renounce their faith.
>
> Presently we have sick ones among our imprisoned relatives who are at the point of death. Our martyred brethren—Khmara of Kulunda, Lanby of Novosibirsk, Kucherenko of Nikolaevsk and others—died after interrogation in camps and prisons. They followed the path of suffering and were faithful to God to the end.

The CPR, under the leadership of Lidiia Vins, mother of Georgii Vins, planned to inform the Soviet government, Russian Christians, and the rest of the world about the plight of prisoners. Although they had to carry out all their proceedings with intense secrecy, the council compiled lists of Christian prisoners to circulate in their own country and the West.

One CPR document issued in 1969 states that more than five hundred dissident Baptists were arrested from 1961 to November, 1969—primarily presbyters and preachers.

While imprisonments of believers were not massive, the communist authorities daily harassed and discriminated against Christians everywhere. In the spring of 1964, an open letter from the church of Barnaul records the following persecutions against Christians:

April 12, 1964:
Druzhinniki and Komsomol members disrupted a service at the home of Yakov Abramovich Pauls, 13 Agrarnaia Street. They frightened the children, made a scene, photographed and counted those assembled.

April 19, 1964:
Twenty-five *druzhinniki* with tape recorders and cameras entered the home of Pavel Ivanovich Klimontov, 9 Yadernaia Street.

April 30, 1964:
Representatives of the Society of Barnaul committed outrages and shouted at the time of preaching in the apartment of Yakov Avgustovich Mantai.

May 2, 1964:
A holiday worship service held at the home of Antonina Mikhailovna Miniakova, 37A Kanifolnyi Passage, was at-

tended by Christians from other cities. Police officers and the KGB conducted an assault, pulling people out of the house by their arms, dragging them by the hair, etc. During the day when everyone sat down to lunch, the police broke in the doors and windows.

In places of business at this time, civil cases were conducted against the Bogomiachikov family and for the second time against many members of the church and against workers in a chemical fiber factory, including Yakov Yakovlevich Bil, who was taken away to court.

Through every lawful channel, Christians in Barnaul and across Russia tried to make their desperate situation known. They pled with their own government to enforce clauses already in the Soviet constitution and laws that would halt persecution and ensure religious freedom. Members of the *Initsiativniki* repeatedly reminded Soviet authorities of the Leninist principle of separation of church and state.

Proceeding a bold step further, *Initsiativniki* leaders Gennadii Kriuchkov and Georgii Vins asked that Soviet legislation be revised to be more equitable to Christians. They claimed that the 1929 legislation enacted under Stalin contradicted original Leninist principles of religious freedom.

From Barnaul and other cities, Christians dispatched signed telegrams to the Soviet government. Local postal officials in Barnaul frequently insisted they must first examine a telegram's contents before they would send it. Often, postal officials ruled the contents of Christians' telegrams "subversive." When the post office refused to accept the telegrams, the persistent believers attempted to send another telegram—a complaint to the Ministry of Communications, asking why telegrams sent by Christians were not reaching the government!

Their telegrams unacknowledged, the Barnaul Christians secretly compiled longer letters—which they duplicated when they could—that carefully and convincingly documented persecution of believers in their congregation and across Russia. Engineer Yurii Mikhalkov kept a meticulous diary of the persecutions of the Barnaul church. While Mikhalkov was in prison, others kept the record current.

While they still thought reform within the AUCECB was possible, the *Initsiativniki* addressed appeals to AUCECB leaders in Moscow. Eventually, most of the *Initsiativniki* gave up hope of reunification with the AUCECB and in September, 1965, formed their own separate union—the Council of Churches of Evangelical Christians-Baptists (CCECB). The CCECB most frequently addressed its appeals to the source of its persecution—the Soviet government itself. The pattern usually went as follows: First the Christians complained to the local authorities, the immediate instruments of their persecution. But the customary answer to their appeals was further repression by the local police. Next they addressed their complaints to regional authorities; then to the national Council of Religious Affairs in Moscow; then to the Supreme Soviet; and finally to Nikita Khrushchev and later to Leonid Brezhnev himself.

When the Christians received no help from highest authorities of their own government, they turned to the West—even though they were aware of the animosity of the Soviet government toward citizens who dare to air internal disagreements beyond the borders of Russia. In desperation, the believers dispatched documents to the United Nations, to which the U.S.S.R. belongs.

In one document addressed to the United Nations, the believers noted that "this document is also being sent to twenty-four Soviet government officials and organizations, including Communist Party Secretary Brezhnev, Premier Kosygin, the Supreme Court of the U.S.S.R., the Union of Writers of the U.S.S.R., the department of history and theory of atheism at Moscow State University, several state publishing houses, and the Museum of the History of Religion and Atheism in Leningrad."

Since they often had difficulty obtaining duplicating materials in Russia, the Christians could often send only one copy of a document to the West. Consequently, in a typical document addressed to the United Nations, the believers ask, "In view of the fact that we do not have the possibility of doing so, we ask that the present appeal be reproduced and sent to all the above-named international organizations, and that the copies be considered authentic."

But no matter how doggedly they tried, the Christians knew they could not consider their mail campaign a success. Nothing had changed. A government commission still had not come to investigate the death of Khmara. The five men sentenced unjustly in 1963 still suffered in prison. In May, 1964, the new presbyter of the Barnaul congregation, Yakov Bil, had been arrested and taken away to court. Places of business conducted new civil cases against believers. Between the springs of 1963 and 1964, the police conducted ten major house searches and meeting disruptions.

The presbyter and deacons of the Barnaul church gathered in the spring of 1964 to pray and seek God's guidance. Across Russia the situation seemed to be growing more grim for Christians. For example, in the first issue of *Kommunist* in 1964, Leonid Ilichev, Khrushchev's chairman of the Ideological Commission of the Central Committee, had written a strident article urging that antireligious activities be increased.

After much prayer, the Christians sensed God leading them to take a bold step. The eldest deacon asked soberly, "Who among us will go to Moscow to protest the injustices—the laws being broken at our expense?"

One elderly deacon and twenty younger men and women were selected for the delegation—a bold step for the believers who had never before taken their appeals directly to the Kremlin. Solemnly, the twenty-one agreed to place themselves in the jaws of the lion. Their only protection would be the God of Daniel.

The Christians planned to leave Barnaul on Saturday, May 16, 1964, to fly to Moscow—1,800 miles away. They would try to see government officials on Monday morning. This meant they would be absent from their jobs and perhaps dismissed when they returned. But they had to take the risk, since it was impossible to request prior permission to be absent. If the local authorities had any inkling of their real mission—to protest at the Presidium—they knew they would never get past the city limits.

On Monday, May 18, the twenty-one Christians presented themselves at the reception room of the Presidium of the Supreme Soviet of the U.S.S.R. in Moscow. They were not received there but routed to the Office for the Affairs of Religious Cults. To their surprise, an official there received them cordially and assured them that all their problems would be solved if they would just return quietly to Barnaul. He spoke so soothingly that Ivan D., the elderly leader of the delegation, was convinced he was sincere.

The other twenty believers were skeptical. They knew from experience that their case could easily be forgotten or delegated to unsympathetic local communist authorities. They realized that assurances of help could swiftly turn to angry retaliation by the time they returned. They distrusted ambiguous Soviet laws that provided enough latitude for authorities to act as they wished.

They felt compelled to press their case further. Grigorii L. explains, "We remembered our brothers and sisters in Barnaul suffering persecution only because they were believers. We thought of our five brothers still in prison. We had not come only on our own behalf or even just to represent the unregistered congregation from Barnaul. We believed that we spoke for all the suffering Christians of Russia. God had helped us this far. We could not turn back."

The elderly leader of the delegation returned home to Barnaul. The other twenty Christians gathered to pray and plan their next step. Already their strategy had been bold. Any further protest could easily mean prison.

"We faced that possibility realistically," Grigorii remembers. "That morning we each asked ourselves, Am I willing to die for Christ? Is there anything in my heart preventing fellowship between me and any other Christian, or between me and God? Am I willing to do anything that the Lord asks? Am I willing to give my life?"

The next morning the Christians walked to the Kremlin and again presented themselves at the prestigious Presidium—the executive council of the Supreme Soviet of the federal government.

Two days later the twenty believers returned home to Barnaul—safe and jubilant. The officials had promised to conduct a "full investigation of the situation of Christians in Barnaul."

1. Michael Bourdeaux, *Religious Ferment* (New York: St. Martin's Press, 1968) p. 67.

11

Interlude

As PROMISED, AN OFFICIAL COMMISSION from the Kremlin visited Barnaul one month later and conducted an investigation.

Comrade Puzin, chairman of the Council for the Affairs of Religious Cults in Moscow, presented an account of the commission's findings to an all-union conference of his colleagues on June 25, 1964:

> Recently a group of twenty-one Evangelical Christian and Baptist believers came to the Council for the Affairs of Religious Cults. All but two of them were under thirty. They had left their work and families and flown from Barnaul to Moscow. They brought a complaint addressed to Nikita S. Khrushchev concerning the crude violation of the law by the town authorities with respect to the believers. "From 1962 onwards," the appeal says, "we have been subjected to constant cruel persecutions: arrests and trials, threats and KGB interrogations, dismissals from work, fines, and continual attacks by the police and *druzhinniki* upon our peaceful services."
>
> The council quickly informed the Central Committee of the Communist Party of the Soviet Union about this com-

plaint, and it was decided to send two representatives of the council to the Altai area. The facts set out by the believers in their complaint were upheld. For several years the local authorities had been carrying out illegal reprisals against religious organizations and believers. . . .

The Party Central Committee always has and always will demand a "sensitive, careful attitude" towards believers. "It is all the more foolish and harmful," it says in the Central Committee Decree of 1954, "to place certain Soviet citizens under political suspicion because of their religious convictions."

This honest statement by Puzin, an influential communist, heartened the Barnaul believers, whose pleas for justice had been so long ignored.

Among other concessions, the commission agreed that Khmara had been tortured by government prison officials; and tacitly admitting that they had committed a crime, they secretly agreed to pay a pension to Khmara's wife and family. The superintendent of the prison where Khmara had been tortured was suspended.

But the commission, and especially local authorities, would not admit publicly that they had treated Khmara unjustly. In fact, lectures were arranged at some places in Barnaul to deny that Khmara had been murdered and to discredit the account the Baptists were spreading. Communist Party newspapers squelched reports of Khmara's murder as rumor and alleged that Khmara died from pneumonia. Party propagandists described the Khmara case as a "fabrication by the Baptists intended to slander Soviet justice."

Ten Christians from the delegation who had traveled to Moscow in May had lost their jobs when they returned. Now the commission allowed these people to return to their former jobs, except Petr Gibert, who was not reinstated as radio monitor of territorial broadcasting. The commission also halted criminal proceedings by a factory against the new presbyter Yakov Bil and returned fines to several believers.

Seven months later, the Christians rejoiced when the five men who had been sentenced in 1963—Dmitrii Miniakov, Yurii Mikhalkov, Grigorii Lebedev, Artur Shtertser, and Iosif Budimer were released by the Presidium of the Supreme Court of the RSFSR "on account of the absence of the essence of crime" and even given financial compensation to cover their time in prison. Jubilantly, the Christians planned celebrations to mark the homecomings of their imprisoned brethren. They also invited believers from across the country.

The enraged local authorities groped for arguments to intimidate the Christians. "Aren't you ashamed to prepare a celebration for a person who has been a prisoner? It is not allowed . . . it is indecent. . . ." They questioned some of the believers at their jobs and tried to extract promises that they would not attend—but to no avail.

"How can I stay home?" Petr K. replied when Communist Party officials questioned him at the tractor factory where he worked. "These five men are my brothers. If you have a son who has been in the army, wouldn't you welcome him with a party when he comes home?"

The Christians went directly to the prison on the days the men were released. They stood outside the gray prison walls, their arms laden with bouquets of flowers (even in winter) for the prisoners.

When the prisoners emerged from the prison gates, their own families—many in tears—were the first to touch them. But the Christians of Barnaul considered themselves one family, and soon they almost smothered the prisoners with embraces and showered them with flowers. Then they paraded them home royally, often accompanied by the youth orchestra.

After all five men were finally released, the Christians held a thanksgiving service. Because their release was officially sanctioned, the Christians were reluctantly permitted the unusual privilege of using the Barnaul registered church for the meeting. But even this building could not contain the more than 500 Christians from all parts of Russia who came to welcome their brothers. The crowd flowed outside the door. "Inside we stood so close that it was hard to find a place to put our feet," one of the deacons remembers.

The service lasted from 10:00 A.M. until late that night. With tears the five men thanked the Christians for "tying to them in prayer." His testimony punctuated by exclamations of joy and gratitude from the congregation, each prisoner recounted how God had sustained him during his confinement. Through the five missionaries some other inmates and even one prison official had been converted to Christ.

To welcome the five prisoners, the Christians sang:

> Welcome, our brothers in suffering.
> We greet you sincerely in peace.
> You lovingly carried to others
> The light and truth of God's word.
>
> The world you met was hostile,
> Branding with mocking disgrace,
> The love you gave to others
> Was countered with hate and disgust.
>
> You firmly and meekly went forward
> Possessing God's light in yourselves,
> Faithfully serving Jesus,
> Knowing his victory in strife.

By a path that is narrow and thorny,
Over mountains of sorrow and grief,
You continued to love in your spirit,
Not looking behind on your loss.

You languished in prison and exile,
Acquainted with suffering and chains.
Your treatment so cruel, so vile,
Inflicted much torture and shame.

We will never forget you, no, never,
Our bearers of Christ's holy name.
Your courage will always be cherished,
And we'll praise God together forever.

The children recited a long poem to commemorate the men's return:

Barren land, severe and cruel,
Sad and desolate is distant Vorkuta*
Your iron chains now grip
Christ's faithful witnesses banished from the south.

O Northland, cruel and dreary,
From the sufferers you hold, from ministers of God,
You will hear no curses.
But they will warm winter's cold and deathly embrace
With loving words and sincere heart.

And helpless are your icy blizzards
To quench God's flame within their hearts,
Nor will the might of your barbed-wire fences
Overpower and defeat the Spirit of God.

Your arctic nature so cruel, so harsh,
Dead tundra 'midst the mighty forests,
Like all of Russia's great expanse,
Will hear the witness of Christ.

*An infamous prison in Russia's arctic region.

O Northland, look! In your barren vastness
Already grows the Gospel seed.
Your downtrodden and abandoned wasteland
Will yield in time a rich harvest.

The day will come when Almighty God will order:
"Enough, far North! Set your prisoners free!
The spring has come, great crops are growing.
Give of your sons to labor in the fields."

The chains will fall; the bonds will soon break.
And precious freedom Christ's soldiers will receive
Endued with might by the Spirit of power.
The Word of Truth will reach to all the earth.

Like all returning prisoners, the Christians were allotted three months after their discharge to find jobs. During this time, the five men took time to visit churches beyond Barnaul to fortify other Christians who might soon face suffering.

When the three months had passed, the five Christians discovered they could not readily find jobs. Even if the authorities had officially released them and recompensed them financially for their months in prison—an admission that the accusations against them were unfounded—the stigma of their Christianity remained.

For example, the authorities would not allow Yurii Mikhalkov to return to his job as an engineer because they considered the position irreconcilable with "unscientific Christianity." Although Yurii protested, he was refused; instead he was assigned to sweep streets near the university where he had formerly studied (see photo section).

Deeply disappointed, Yurii resolved to use his demotion as an opportunity. His professors had considered him a promising student and had been proud of his academic achievement. Now when they passed the street where he swept with his broom, Yurii spoke to them of his faith in Christ.

The Barnaul Christians had been greatly encouraged by the commission's investigation and Chairman Puzin's objective report in June, 1964. In October, when Khrushchev retired, the intensity of the national antireligious campaign appeared to ease—evidently on orders from Moscow. Some Soviet newspapers even publicly criticized Khrushchev's brutal excesses.

But during the following months, hope diminished. The local party officials in Barnaul, who had never conceded responsibility for unjust actions, seemed more prepared than ever to intensify repressions against Christians in their city. Puzin's chiding report had embarrassed them.

For example, the regional newspaper *Altai Truth* had published a stinging article entitled "Sectarian Stench." It said, "We cannot tolerate Baptist trickery, just as we do not tolerate hooligans, thieves, parasites, and other enemies of our society. Let the ground slip from under the sectarians' feet too." The article exhorted citizens not to reeducate believers but to expose them. "If even the slightest hint of tolerance is shown towards sectarians, workers may justly regard this as encouraging the fanatics."

The chairman of Barnaul's Altai Area Industrial Executive Committee, Comrade Andrianov, said, "We have liquidated almost all the religious hotbeds here. We are not like other regions. We wage an energetic struggle with the believers, and we shall not—repeat, not—have a prayer house opened here. Sectarians are parasites, rogues, and criminals, and they should be sentenced."

During 1965, some believers felt that perhaps the time was right to again present their case to Moscow. Possibly Kremlin officials would at last try to revise repressive legislation and edicts.

In June, 1965, Yurii Mikhalkov and Petr Gibert joined two delegations of about forty Christians from unregistered churches across Russia to travel to the governing Presidium in Moscow.

Gibert and Mikhalkov carried petitions representing the entire unregistered Barnaul congregation, as well as requests to be reinstated to their own jobs. But their delegation was received only by Comrade Kopenkin, the assistant chief of reception. The Presidium did not answer the Christians' petitions.

On August 16-21, a nationwide delegation of a hundred people from unregistered churches in Russia traveled once more to the Presidium of the Supreme Soviet. Yurii Mikhalkov was again chosen to represent the Barnaul congregation. Procurator General R. A. Rudenko received the delegation in the registration waiting room and lectured them for forty minutes, telling them to disperse. Rudenko claimed he did not have authority to act upon their complaints.

At their urgent request, five delegates later met with the chairman of the Presidium of the Supreme Soviet, A. E. Mikoyan, on September 22. The delegates presented Mikoyan with documents recording typical injustices perpetrated against believers. They also presented sixteen other documents reporting attacks upon believers, destruction of prayer houses, and other reprisals suffered by unregistered Christians across the country. Mikoyan promised that freedom of conscience would be restored in the Soviet Union.

The Christians returned home with new hope. But as time passed, their complaints were ignored, and to make matters worse, just before the 23rd Communist Party Congress met that spring, Article 142 of the penal code was amended on March 18, 1966, and in some aspects made more harsh.

The amended Article 142 made it illegal for members of religious groups to refuse to register, to organize religious meetings for children, or to print and distribute religious literature. All of these prohibitions struck hard at the Baptists.

Interestingly, Article 142 also made it a crime, punishable by as much as three years' imprisonment, to "refuse to accept citizens at work or into an educational institution; to dismiss them from work or to exclude them from an educational institution; to deprive them of privileges or advantages guaranteed by law; or similarly to place material restrictions on the rights of citizens as a result of their religious adherence."

However, while authorities readily invoke certain clauses of Article 142 to prosecute Christians, it does not appear that the section of Article 142 guaranteeing the rights of believers has ever been used.[1]

In desperation, delegates from the recently formed Council of Churches of Evangelical Christians—Baptists (CCECB) planned another trip to Moscow on May 16, 1966, shortly after the revolutionary May Day holiday. This time five hundred delegates from CCECB churches gathered not far from the Kremlin. They met in *Staraia Ploshchad* (Old Square), across from the Communist Party Central Committee building and only a few blocks from the notorious Liubianka prison, where the grim statue of Feliks Dzerzhinskii stands sentry. The crowd of believers had come from 130 towns across the USSR.

About eleven of the delegates were from Barnaul.

People in Old Square stared as the Christians clustered together. Nearby was a monument peaked by an Orthodox cross honoring Russian marines who died in Bulgaria in the 1800s fighting the Turks for the "salvation of the Slavs." At first passersby assumed the delegation must be a tour group. They could not believe that a protest demonstration—even a peaceful one—would occur in the shadow of the Kremlin, in front of the Central Committee building of the Communist Party, headquarters of the most powerful men in the Soviet Union. Such a preposterous event hadn't happened since before the Revolution.

But the Christians had come to protest—peaceably. They carried a document which they hoped to present to Leonid Brezhnev, chairman of the Central Committee. The document requested recognition of CCECB congregations and asked that members of these churches be allowed to hold a national congress. The document implored the government to halt persecution of believers and to freely permit them to pass on their faith to their own children.

All day Monday, May 16, the five hundred Christians waited near the Central Committee building. They prayed, sang, and encouraged each other with the Scriptures. When they prayed, they knelt on the grass or sidewalks. During the day they fasted. That night, they opened their suitcases filled with food from home and ate. Curious crowds and foreign newsmen gathered to watch.

The next morning about one hundred Christians from the registered Moscow Baptist Church joined the reformers. This sign of solidarity strengthened the protesters. They all waited together as the day wore on and the spring sunshine turned to rain.

After noon on May 17 the vigil was brutally broken. Officials, soldiers, and police surrounded the delegation. While astonished onlookers stood by, the police hurled themselves at the believers. They struck at the protesters with bottles and clubs, tore clothes, and pulled hair.

Finally the police took the delegates to the city stables—one place large enough to contain the crowd of Christians. Inside the arena, the bedraggled, battered Christians rejoiced that they were at least together. They soon started to sing and pray. Curious bystanders gathered to watch the Gospel service. Later the police came with vehicles and said, "We're taking you to a better place." The Christians soon found themselves in various Moscow prisons.

The delegates were fingerprinted, despite Yurii Mikhalkov's objection that "We did not come to Moscow to be examined by the KGB." Most of the Christians were eventually allowed to return home, but some went to prison. On May 19, CCECB leaders Georgii Vins and Gennadii Kriuchkov were also arrested and held in the Lefortovo Prison. From the Barnaul delegation, Evald Gauf was sentenced to twelve days for petitioning to be reinstated to his electrician's job, and Yakov Abramovich Pauls received the same punishment on May 27. Yurii— out of prison less than eighteen months—was now sentenced to a two-year prison term for participating in the demonstration that had been only a peaceful protest on the part of the Christians.

Leonid Brezhnev probably never saw the believers' written request for official recognition. And the persecution which Puzin's report had temporarily abated continued unchecked by Moscow.

1. Michael Bourdeaux, "Baptists and Other Protestants," *Religious Minorities in the Soviet Union* (Minority Rights Group, August, 1973, p. 18.)

12

The Fallout

CIVIL RIGHTS CRUSADES such as the May, 1966, protest at the nation's capital severely embarrassed and also enraged communist authorities back home. Chagrined officials in Barnaul felt the sting of failure when they considered the situation of Christians in their city. The registered church, although not particularly active, remained open. But it was the unregistered church that the authorities worried about most. Not only had the congregation refused to disband, but it thrived in spite of their pressure. And it was not even technically violating Article 142 of the penal code by "refusing to register." Repeatedly the congregation had requested permission to register, but only according to conditions they considered constitutional.

Thus, the local authorities renewed their campaign to reeducate believers. They formed more committees to organize and supervise atheistic work. They distributed handbooks instructing atheistic workers how to convert Christians. They showed atheistic films such as *The Confession, Armageddon,* and *Beyond the Darkness.* They presented antireligious dramas and even an antireligious

144

ballet. Atheistic literature was distributed widely across the city, and citizens were encouraged to read publications such as *Nauka i Religiia* (Science and Religion).

They also dispatched workers to visit Christian homes, prayer meetings, and places where believers worked. They instructed them to gain the confidence of believers and "gradually win them from their religion." Agitators from the atheistic society Znanie came to conduct anti-God lectures at clubs and in factories.

But many atheistic workers found believers baffling. "It is hard to find the key to unlock the soul of these *veruiushchie,*" one agitator often grumbled.

Puzin's report back in 1964 had contended that atheistic education was not being conducted correctly:

> Our comrades visited numerous factories in Barnaul, and none of them are carrying on educational work with sectarians. The secretary of the party committee at Factory #521, Comrade Yegorov—a former member of the Altai area party committee—stated, "It's hopeless to try to reeducate believers. They should be dismissed from work and indicted." The president of the trade union in Barnaul, Comrade Yefimov—a former KGB official—openly stated, "It's useless talking to them." He said he "felt like strangling them."

Pressure at their jobs was not new to Barnaul Christians. Sometimes the attack was only verbal. In other instances, persecution was brutally physical.

Leonid H., Fedor R., and Boris L. all worked at a sewing machine factory in the northwest section of the city. Each of the men earned about 100 rubles a month. Although the wage was meager, all three had large families and felt thankful for steady jobs.

When they were hired, the factory supervisor had told

the other employees, "Watch out for those three. They're Baptists!" The supervisor, a man determined to rise in the ranks of the Communist Party, had also at times instructed other workers to "make it uncomfortable for the Baptists so they'll leave. It doesn't look good on the factory record having *three* of them here!"

One day while Leonid worked by a machine located under a balcony, another workman purposely dropped a heavy hammer that fell within inches of where Leonid stood. Another time a workman shoved a metal cylinder from a balcony that almost hit Boris. Convinced that the cylinder had not fallen by accident, Boris confronted his assailant. The worker said sheepishly, "I had to. One of the party members told me I must do this as an assignment. I had no alternative. I have nothing against you personally, but if I refused, I might lose my job."

In other instances, the Christian men felt their trousers on fire, only to discover that lighted cigarettes had been purposely stuffed into their pockets. Leonid still carries a scar from the day a worker "accidentally" pressed a hot piece of metal against his skin.

At some factories persecution swelled to the point that Christians felt their lives in danger. Several of the Christian men complained to regional labor authorities that "physical violence against Christians violates Soviet legislation." The Christians cited the clause in Article 142 of the amended penal code protecting the right of religious persons.

"But what can I do if all of the workers find your religion traitorous?" one official shrugged. "After all, the collective is hardly likely to make a mistake."

"Our supervisor constantly tried to trick us into saying something against the Communist Party or against the government that could be used as a pretext for dismissing us," Fedor remembers. "But the three of us supported and guarded each other. We spoke cautiously and always tried to be the best workers in the whole factory."

One time Boris's foreman threatened to incriminate him. "It's easy," he laughed. "I'll just put some parts from the sewing machine inside your locker and ask the authorities to search it. They'll think you stole the parts."

"The man who digs a hole usually falls into it," Boris replied.

Several weeks later the foreman, who also worked as a fisherman on weekends, was arrested when he pilfered some heavy thread from the factory to make a fishing net.

Surprisingly, Boris was chosen to serve on the factory jury to judge the foreman. Asked for his verdict, Boris answered, "As a Christian, I forgive the foreman for his crime because God has forgiven him. But, comrades, if the foreman knew God, he would not have committed this crime in the first place."

Several times the three Christians were eligible for production awards and end-of-the-year bonuses. Fedor recalls with a rueful smile, "Before I became a Christian, I used to regularly receive production awards. I still wear the wrist watch I was once awarded. But since I became a Christian and worked harder than ever, I have never received an award."

Leonid remembers an instance when he was indisputably eligible for an award and the whole factory knew it. The supervisor felt forced to list Leonid's name in the newspaper, but purposely misspelled his last name to save the embarrassment of publicly commending a Christian.

As part of the campaign to reeducate believers and warn other citizens against religion, crude posters were plastered in factories, clubs, and public places throughout the city.

In the factory where Vadim M. worked, enlarged photos of three Christians who had been sentenced to prison appeared on the bulletin board. Wings and halos had been drawn on one of the photos. On another a horse collar had been added with the words "Enslaved Christian." On the third, the face had been mutilated so that the man looked as if he had leprosy. Lettered crudely across the photos were the words, "These are Baptists. They sacrifice their children."

Vadim protested to the factory foreman, "You know what you have written is not true. God will make you remove these pictures."

"They're never coming down!" the foreman shouted, shoving Vadim aside. "As for you, it would be better if you came crawling to work drunk than preaching about God!"

One night when all the other workers were gone, Vadim removed the photos from the factory, took them home, and photographed them. He rehung them early the next morning before work.

The next day he sent the photos to authorities in Moscow. He enclosed a letter that said, "This caliber of propaganda is *nekulturno*—uncultured!" Vadim acknowledged the constitutional right of local authorities to freedom of antireligious propaganda, but he also reminded the officials that the Communist Party had stated that "antireligious propaganda should not be insulting to the feelings of believers."

In a few days, the astonished factory foreman received orders from Moscow. "Immediately remove the *nekulturnaia* propaganda in your factory," the directive demanded.

As a result of Puzin's 1964 report, local authorities in Barnaul began to place more emphasis on conducting communist ideological meetings at places where Christians worked.

At Aleksei K.'s factory, the atheistic lecturer was also a Communist Party member. "Believers are generally backward people—in some cases, mentally retarded," he asserted. "Christians are opposed to cultural events. For example, they do not allow their children to go to movies. Baptists are poor workers and cannot be trusted."

At the end of the meeting, Aleksei stood. "You have spent the whole lecture criticizing Christians, and I am the only Christian at this factory," he said. "But in our factory, as you all know, we have many drunks. You have not said one word about drunken workers, their absence from work, or their low production standards, which slow socialist construction."

Although Christians were obligated to attend atheistic lectures at work, they did not always feel obliged to listen to slanderous attacks against them without replying. In the factory where Nadezhda S. worked, the lecturer charged that Christians sacrifice their children. He had not read the Bible, but he had seen a version of the story of Abraham and Isaac in his atheist instructor's manual. He also knew that Christian doctrine teaches that Christ "shed his blood for the forgiveness of sins." Further, he was acquainted with Romans 12: 1—which commands a Christian to offer his body as a "living sacrifice" unto God. With this evidence, the lecturer confidently presented his case.

Nadezhda could stay silent no longer. "Please, comrade—may I interrupt for a moment?" she said. "I have ten children. I have been awarded the title 'Heroine Mother' by the state," she announced proudly.

"Most of the Christians in our congregation have large families," she continued. "Please show me one Christian parent who has killed his child. We Christians love and care for our families. It is not we who sacrifice children—it is the many Soviet citizens who approve and practice abortion! Why do you not speak against them, comrade?"

At one lecture the atheist propagandist spoke for an hour on "Evidence Against the Existence of God." At last he asked the weary audience, "Are there any questions?"

Yevgenii G., a believer, rose. "If there is no God, why is it necessary for you to speak against him? If he doesn't exist, isn't it foolish for us to speak of him at all—much less to speak against him?"

Frequently at atheistic lectures, the sympathy of the audience was swayed to the side of the bold believers who refused to listen silently while lies were propagated about them. Sometimes curious nonbelievers questioned the Christians about their faith. Consequently, atheistic lectures often paved the way for an opportunity to witness.

Often, the atheistic lecturers themselves appeared to find their task tedious and boring. Frequently, articles appeared in the Soviet Press rebuking atheistic agitators for their flagging zeal. The following article entitled "For an Effective Atheist Propaganda" appeared on page 1 of *Pravda.*

Atheistic propaganda reaches its target only when it is conducted systematically and followed through. As things are now, in some regions . . . a misconceived practice has taken hold. The agitators intensify their atheistic movement during the religious holidays and then forget about it. Such one-shot campaigns in a complex and delicate matter of this kind are particularly not to be tolerated.[1]

Another front-page *Pravda* article proclaimed:

And above all, each Communist Party member must be a militant atheist. We cannot put up with instances when some Party members and *Komsomoltsy* themselves direct religious ceremonies, as happened in Kemerovskaya, Orlovskaya, and Nikolayevskaya oblasts. Training propagandists in scientific atheism is a top priority in upgrading the forms and techniques of atheist education. . . . Shaping the scientific world view and uprooting religious prejudices is one of the combat missions of all ideological workers and agencies of mass information and propaganda.[2]

Openly, communist officials tried to dissuade Christians through atheistic education. Covertly, they tried to destroy the church from within by soliciting informers.

Before his conversion, Kondrat Solomonovich Rudi spent ten years in various prison camps for robbery and hooliganism. In 1965, he started to attend the unregistered church meetings in Barnaul, where he was converted and later became a member.

In late 1965, the supervisor of the foundry shop of the Transmash factory summoned Rudi. Two men, who did not identify themselves, told Rudi they wanted to chat with him. During the conversation, they commented, "Do you know that there are spies and saboteurs at those Baptist meetings you attend?"

Rudi dismissed the accusation. "You have attended our meetings," he said. "You know we only preach the Gospel of Christ."

During the fall of 1965 and through the following spring, the supervisor summoned Rudi approximately nineteen times for conversations and each time asked him to be an informer against the unregistered Christians. The officials proposed that Rudi would simply continue going to the meetings as before and report everything to the KGB. "You will be paid well," the officer promised. "If you cooperate, you could become a KGB agent. We need people who are honest, who have high moral character and don't drink."

At first, the officials simply suggested proposals in a friendly fashion. Then they fiercely threatened Rudi during sessions held at the chemical fiber works and the cotton textile works.

But Rudi resisted firmly, refusing to betray the believers. In fact, as a precaution he told the whole church about the KGB's invitation to join their ranks. Steadfastly, the Barnaul congregation supported Rudi and prayed God would give him strength to refuse. Several of the Christians had been through the same ordeal with the KGB themselves and knew what their brother was suffering.

After almost nine months of coercion by the KGB, Rudi still refused to yield. On June 18, 1966, the procurator of the investigative division of the procurator's office of Altai Territory, A. Rylov, conducted a search at Rudi's house. (Eventually, on February 14, 1967, Rudi was arrested and held for five days.)

When Rudi still refused to cooperate, the KGB tried to pin the informant job on another Christian—Aluiz Aleksandrovich Shtertser.

On July 28, 1966, Aluiz was summoned from the Polytechnical Institute, where he was repairing parquet floors, for a conversation with Senior KGB Officer Dmitrii Stepanovich Gribok.

On August 4, Shtertser was again taken to Officer Gribok. The KGB continued to harass him that fall. Even when he lay ill in the Stroigas Hospital on October 25,

1966, Officer Gribok visited him, urging Shtertser to reconsider becoming an informer. After this, he was approached three more times by the KGB, but he flatly refused their offers.

When the KGB could not persuade believers inside the church to act as informers, they tried to infiltrate false believers into the church.

Yasha R., a member of the Barnaul church, remembers a man who came to call at his apartment. "I am a Christian," the man insisted. "I have just moved to Barnaul and I'm delighted to find other believers." Later, the man offered, "I have a hidden press. If you have anything you want printed, I'll be happy to help you."

Although the offer of the press seemed suspicious, the Christians welcomed the newcomer into their congregation and even invited him to preach. He gave a stirring sermon on the Parable of the Ten Virgins. He vigorously sang hymns. However, he avoided praying aloud at all costs.

But the presbyter insisted, "We are going to pray, and we want you, brother, to lead us in prayer."

Eventually the Christians discovered that the man was an informer—planted by the KGB. Over the years, they learned to test people whom they were not sure they could trust. "Will you lead us aloud in prayer?" they would ask.

Concurrently with their campaign to destroy the church from within, the Barnaul authorities were frowning on a new meeting site the Christians had selected. On August 15, 1965, Evald Gustavovich Gauf, his wife and children, and Yekaterina Fedorovna Shirobokova, a widow with one daughter, had signed as owners of a brick house at 22 Strelochnaia Street. With financial help from the other Christians, the Gaufs and Shirobokova had purchased the house for use as a *molitvennyi dom*— house of prayer. Although the purchase was legal, the owners were unable for six months to obtain registration to reside there—a procedure usually routine and rapid.

Gauf and several of the other believers petitioned the Territorial Executive Committee in Barnaul to investigate illegal government interference preventing registration of the house as a residence. The Christians asked to see the president of this committee, Comrade S. V. Kalchenko.

On Friday, November 26, the whole church gathered at the committee office in Barnaul. The Christians who entered the building first were thrown out.

The next day, about two hundred Christians returned. All day they stood in the courtyard, until *druzhinniki* tore through the crowd and thrust them out.

Monday, Comrade Kalchenko and his deputies grudgingly received a small delegation. The Christians requested permission to register Gauf's house. Grateful for the rare opportunity to present their case to a communist official, they also petitioned that persecutions and criminal proceedings against believers be stopped—not only in Barnaul but also in Slavgorod, Nekrasovo, Orlovka, Aleksandrovka, and other villages of the territory.

The Executive Committee answered harshly with fines and arrests. Anatolii Kharitonovich Liukhtinen was summoned to a civil court at the radio factory where he had worked for ten years. For participating in the delegation, he was fined and fired. For their participation, Galina Gerasimenko and Mariia Klimakova were also dismissed from work for six months. In February, 1967—almost a year and a half later—Yakov Bil was charged under Article 142 of the RSFSR penal code with organizing the delegation to the Territorial Executive Committee.

The Christians nevertheless continued to meet at Gauf's house during the winter of 1965.

Finally, the angry authorities accused Gauf, "You are conducting church next door to a school with ten grades. You could corrupt the students! The Territorial Executive Committee and the court of the Railroad Region have handed down a new decision," the authorities announced. "Your house will be demolished, and a multilevel residential building will be constructed in its place."

On March 9, 1966—five years and two months after the registered prayer house had been padlocked—a brigade of *druzhinniki* arrived at Gauf's unregistered prayer house with irons and crowbars. Several Christians were praying inside. The *druzhinniki* broke down the doors, damaged the house, and left.

Eight days later, the Executive Committee sent a brigade, including *druzhinniki* who had been given a holiday to help, to finish the job with a bulldozer. Firetrucks were also dispatched to encircle the house and block the view of passersby.

Gauf's three small children, two elderly ladies, and two retired men, Grigorii Dmitrievich Lebedev and Adolf Mikhailovich Radke, happened to be inside the house this time. The wrecking crew chased them out, and when Radke protested, they bound his arms and placed him on a bus.

The next morning, the whole church gathered at the ruins and prayed. Meanwhile, the authorities circulated a rumor that underneath the house, a cemetery containing bones of babies had been discovered. They termed it irrefutable evidence that the Barnaul Christians had been "sacrificing children."

In a document describing the destruction of their prayer house, the Christians wrote:

> Such actions were a great surprise both to us believers and to the unbelievers of the whole town—and especially to those who were actually present at this operation of brutal violence upon us believers unlike anything done since 1937 [the height of Stalin's purges]. It was the sort of thing you would not believe, even if someone told you about it.
>
> To all the cries of astonishment, the police major, one of the responsible participants in this pogrom, casually remarked, "Don't worry; if Moscow permits it, a bigger house will be built for you on this spot."
>
> One would wish to think that it were not so—that is, that Moscow did not do this folly in the name of the struggle against religion. But how can one think otherwise? Moreover, the ruling of the primary court was confirmed by all appellate courts including the Supreme Court of the U.S.S.R., which until now still has not given any answer to the complaint. . . .
>
> It is difficult to avoid the fact that the courts, police, the press, radio, and all government agencies are obedient executors of the policy of suppressing all religious belief. . . .

On June 21, 1966, Evald Gustavovich Gauf, the owner of the house, was dismissed as a "hooligan" from his iron and cement manufacturing plant Barnaultselinstroi. And to this day (see photo section), only a mound of earth remains at 22 Strelochnaia Street.

1. "For an Effective Atheist Propaganda," *Pravda*, July 27, 1968. (Translated in *Religion in Communist Dominated Areas*, Vol. VII, Nos. 17-18, September 15/30, 1968, p. 163.)

2. "Atheist Education," *Pravda*, September 15, 1972. (Translated in *Religion in Communist Dominated Areas*, Vol. XI, Nos. 7—9, July-August-September, 1972, p. 139.)

13

Bibles and Broadcasts

THE DESTRUCTION of Gauf's prayer house was consistent with the communist campaign against any and all tangible elements of the Christian faith. Another target of long standing has been the Scriptures. Today in Barnaul, it is impossible to buy a Bible or Christian book in any bookstore. This scarcity of Christian literature extends throughout the vast U.S.S.R.

Occasionally people barter for Bibles and Christian books on the black market, but they must often pay as much as half a month's wage (fifty to eighty rubles)—more than most Christians can readily afford.

Bibles have been scarce in Russia for a long time. It wasn't until 1875 that the whole Bible was translated into Russian, and seven more years passed before it was published in any significant amount (20,000 copies). Even then, however, there was little encouragement to own or read the Bible. In fact, the rapid spread of a biblical, evangelical faith which followed the availability of Bibles alarmed the tsarist authorities and resulted in a twenty-year repression of non-Orthodox Christians and no further editions of the Bible.

This growth of evangelical Christianity in the late nineteenth and on into the early twentieth century resulted in an increased demand for Bibles. In addition to the few which were printed with the authorization of tsarist officials, the British and Foreign Bible Society brought some Bibles into Russia and also printed some there.

The greatest opportunity evangelical Christians ever had came in the ten years immediately following the Bolshevik Revolution of 1917. Ivan Prokhanoff, the ambitious president of the Evangelical Christian Union in Russia, raised American funds to print 60,000 Bibles, 60,000 hymnals, and 15,000 concordances inside Russia.

In 1957, the Soviet government allowed the AUCECB to print approximately 10,000 Bibles; in 1968, 20,000 Bibles; and in 1974, 20,000 New Testaments. During this time the Russian Orthodox Church and a few other groups, such as the Armenian Orthodox Church and the Latvian Lutheran Church, were also permitted to print some Scriptures.

Statistics reveal that more Bibles have been produced in Soviet Russia under communism than were printed in the hundreds of years of tsarism and Orthodox Church supremacy.

However, in a country of 255 million people, the approximate total of 250,000 authorized Bibles (including New Testaments and portions) since 1956 still amounts to less than one Bible per thousand. Even if one considers only the religious sector of the population—approximately 50 million Russian Orthodox, 6 million

Protestants, and 3.5 million Catholics—only one person out of 240 would receive a Bible.*

To make matters worse, some of the 1957 printing was shipped by the government to Russian emigrants outside the country as proof of Soviet religious freedom.

In 1945, the AUCECB received permission to launch a bimonthly religious journal, *Bratskii Vestnik (Fraternal Herald)*. At present the union is allowed to print only approximately 6,000 copies at a time—enough to supply one copy per AUCECB church, but not enough to supply all Baptists of the U.S.S.R.

While Moscow has severely limited the publication of Bibles and Christian literature, atheistic literature pours lavishly from Soviet presses. The leading atheistic monthly, *Nauki i Religiia,* has a circulation of 300,000 (440,000 in February, 1976). From 1928 to 1940 a total of 140 million copies of antireligious literature (1,832 titles) were printed. After a 19-year lull, authorities renewed this heavy output, launching an all-out campaign in 1959 which continues to the present.[1]

Soviet officials have claimed they must restrict Bible printings because of paper scarcity. Paper, they insist, must be saved for high-priority items. Combating religion is apparently one of those priorities.

In every corner of the Soviet Union, atheistic literature has always been easily obtainable—in fact, impossible to avoid. At every bookstore and kiosk in the city, citizens can readily purchase books such as *What to Tell Your Child About Christmas, Inculcation of Communist Morality, Before*

---

*In comparison, the American Bible Society reported in 1976 that it alone had distributed 981,370,649 Bibles (or portions) in the U.S. since 1956—an average of 4.6 Bibles for each of an estimated 213 million citizens. And this figure is only a fraction of the millions of Bibles produced by U.S. publishing houses.

the Judgment Seat of Science, The Myth of the Immortality of the Soul, and *The Story of a Former Priest.*

Like all churches in Russia, the congregation in Barnaul has always yearned for more Bibles. They have treasured and shared the few Bibles they own. If a Christian book can be found, the believers pass it around until it crumbles. Many families use their turn as an opportunity to copy favorite Scripture passages.

Believers who possessed and circulated Christian literature especially angered communist authorities in Barnaul. Often searches were conducted simultaneously in several Christian homes in order to prevent families from transferring literature to safety during a search. Besides seizing printed materials, police in some instances removed plaques with Scripture inscriptions from the walls and confiscated money and other household items.

An open letter from the church in Barnaul states that the eight months from May to December, 1966, saw repeated searches to find and confiscate religious literature under the pretext of Article 142 of the penal code:

May 24, 1966:
Eight-hour search from two to ten P.M. in the apartment of Yurii Mikhalkov, 28 Molodezhnaia Street, Apartment 63, by Junior Councilor of Justice A. S. Rylov of the Investigative Division, Procurator's Office of Altai Territory.
May 27, 1966:
Search in the home of Nikolai Konstantinovich Gavriushkin, 3 First Keramicheskaia Street, by Investigator Yerin of the Procurator's Office of Altai Territory. . . .
May 27, 1966:
Search and interrogation in the home of Artur Gerbetovich Mantai, 18 Second Rechnaia Street, by Investigator Bobrov of the Procurator's Office of October Region. . . .

May 27, 1966:
Search in the apartment of Yakov Yakovlevich Bil, 47A First Zapadnaia Street, Apartment 11, by Investigator Rylov, of the Procurator's Office of Altai Territory. . . .

June 18, 1966:
Search in the home of Kondrat Solomonovich Rudi, 47A Gorskaia Street, by Procurator Rylov of the Investigative Department of the Procurator's Office, Altai Territory. . . .

December 23, 1966:
Search in the home of Gotlib Genrikhovich Airikh, 29 Second Severozapadnaia Street, by the procurator of the Investigative Division of the Territorial Procurator's Office. . . .

December 23, 1966:
Search in the apartment of Yakov Yakovlevich Bil, 47A Second Zapadnaia Street, Apartment 11, by Procurator Rylov of the Investigative Division of the Procurator's Office of Altai Territory. . . .

December 23, 1966:
Search in the apartment of Evald Gustavovich Gauf, 139 Severozapadnaia Street, Apartment 3, by Senior Investigator Yerin of the Procurator's Office of Altai Territory.

One open letter contains a copy of the report prepared by the police after they searched Evald Gauf's apartment on December 23, 1966:

The search was conducted in observance of Articles 169-171, 176, and 177 of the penal code of the RSFSR for the purpose of seeking literature which encourages nonobservance of legislation on religious cults.

Found in the search:

1. Books of religious poems manufactured by hand in 105 pages, beginning with the poem "Oh, Joy, Joy Will Be There for Redeemed Hearts" and ending with the poem "I Have Come to Know a Wonderful Friend," 22 books in all.

2. Religious poems prepared for binding, 16 books in all.

3. Account of the meeting of representatives of the Council of Churches of Evangelical Christians-Baptists held 23 March 1966 in Moscow, on 18 pages in pink binding.

4. Ordinary notebooks with religious stories, 9 pages.

5. Envelope with the address: Omsk Oblast, Isiol-Kulskii Region, Boevoi.

6. Note with address.

7. Letter from Moldavian SSR from Pavel Buriak on one sheet.

8. Letter from Irma Liust, Pavlodar Oblast, on one sheet.

9. Letter from Edik to Fedia on two sheets.

10. Three photographs.

11. Handwritten address under the heading "Married Life," 11 pages.

12. Writing pad with 188 religious verses.

13. Open letter to the Central Committee of the Communist Party of the Soviet Union.

14. Journal *Vestnik Spaseniia,* No. 2, 1966.

15. Notebook without cover containing religious questions.

16. Aids for the study of the Gospel, 160 pages.

17. Notebook with religious verses.

18. Text in German, 80 pages.

19. Machine for stitching books and two new blocks for pressing them.

20. Brown suitcase.

Signatures of Witnesses
Signature of Investigator, V. Yerin

To supplement their own scarce supplies, Christians in several cities of Russia gratefully received Bibles and Christian literature from Western tourists. At first these gifts seldom reached Barnaul, which was closed to foreigners. But gradually more Bibles filtered through to Siberia. "We prayed, fasted, and asked God to send Christians to our country who would bring Bibles," Igor

L. remembers. "All of us wanted Bibles so desperately that we had to agree among ourselves who should have the first opportunity to own any Bibles we managed to receive. We gave our pastors the first chance."

Mikhail N., who received a Bible from the West, remembers the day it arrived. "I was in the hospital, and no medicine seemed to help me. Every day I was growing weaker. And then one afternoon my wife brought me a Bible that had come to us through tourists visiting Leningrad. The Bible was like a tonic to me, and that day I started to heal!"

The Soviet government viewed the importation of Bibles as a poison, not a tonic. In an article entitled "Undercover of the Gospel" published in *The Leningrad Truth,* the Soviet writer L. Serdobolskaia deplored the "flow of religious literature and tracts into our country" as "one form of ideological diversion." She warned those who print and deliver Christian literature to the Soviet Union, "Don't waste your money, gentlemen slanderers! Your dirty wares will find no takers among Soviet people!"[2]

The famine for written Scripture in Russia made Christians in Barnaul depend deeply on Gospel broadcasts transmitted from foreign radio stations. Presently, eleven Protestant missionary radio stations broadcast religious programming into the U.S.S.R.: Trans World Radio (TWR) from Monaco and Bonaire; Far East Broadcasting Company (FEBC) from Korea, the Philippine Islands, and California; Voice of the Andes from Ecuador; Radio Trans Europe from Portugal; TEAM Radio from Korea; Family Radio Network from Massachusetts; and Radio KICY and Radio KJNP from Alaska.

Religious programs are also broadcast to Russia by the British Broadcasting Corporation, *Deutsche Welle,* Voice of America, Radio Liberty, and Radio Vatican.

The majority of foreign religious programs are broadcast via short wave. Although quality short-wave sets can cost as much as one or two months' wages, an estimated 40 million radio sets with short wave are in use. Even Radio Moscow commonly uses short wave for internal broadcasting.

Radio Moscow also frequently propagates atheism via short wave. In an article entitled "A Light Against the Darkness" from the Tashkent newspaper *Pravda Vostoka* (Truth of the East), the editor-in-chief of the Bukhar Provincial Committee on Radio Communication describes the successful use of radio to implement atheistic education:

> More than two years have passed since we at the Provinces Radio Committee organized a scientific-atheistic council. Its members are party workers, distinguished persons in the field of culture, experienced pedagogues, members of the Znanie Society—people who have a great deal of experience in atheistic work and are expert lecturers. During the last two years they have organized 62 antireligious broadcasts in three languages. During the same period more than 300 reports have been broadcast on how to carry out antireligious activities in various places. And the Provinces Radio presented reviews of new books on atheism, and satires and skits which unmask the reactionary nature of the different religious beliefs.
>
> The program of the Radio Committee includes talks bringing out the significance of the Leninist-atheistic inheritance in the war against anachronistic religious practices.[3]

While freely promulgating atheism, the Soviet government permits no Christian programs to be transmitted within the U.S.S.R. Further, the Soviet government denounces foreign groups which broadcast religious programming into the country. One article entitled "Firebrands" asserts, "In the flood of anti-Soviet propaganda, religious radio programs occupy a big place."[4] Another article from *Nauka i Religiia* describes the foreign stations as "a gigantic spider's web . . . enveloping the world."[5]

Religious broadcasters are accused of promulgating the only philosophy which is "capable of having a mass appeal that is alien to Marxism-Leninism in a communist world outlook,'' according to Boris Maksimovich Marianov, executive secretary of *Nauka i Religiia.*[6]

At the 24th Congress of the Communist Party, Leonid Brezhnev complained:

> We live under an incessant ideological war waged by imperialist propagandists against our land—against the world of socialism. They employ the most refined devices and technical means. All the implements for influencing the mind are found in the hands of the bourgeois: the press, the cinema, the radio are mobilized to mislead people and to instill into them the illusion of nearly paradisiacal life under capitalism and thus slander socialism.

Even though the government discourages its citizens from tuning in to foreign broadcasts, listening to international radio programs remains one of the most popular forms of entertainment in the U.S.S.R. Believers cling to Gospel broadcasts as a spiritual lifeline.

Yakov K., who now has two children of his own, was a teenager when the Gospel broadcasts were first heard in Barnaul. "Some of the Christians in our church discovered broadcasts from radio station FEBC," Yakov remembers. "Before then, they felt radio was an invention of the devil. Now it became like God's voice from heaven. My parents saved rubles and bought a short-wave set. I still remember when we heard the first program. My father wept, because he could not believe that in atheistic Russia he would be able to hear the Gospel every day.

"Now my wife and I and our two children listen. Occasionally the government tries to jam the broadcasts, but usually reception is clear. We regularly listen to FEBC from the Philippine Islands and HLKX from Korea. Often we hear TWR from Monte Carlo and occasionally HCJB from Quito, Ecuador."

The stations plan their schedules for the major population centers in European Russia, which means that in Barnaul, several time zones to the east, it is already late at night when some of the programs are aired. "But we all stay up to listen," says Yakov. "In summer when the reception changes, the broadcasts reach us even later; sometimes we stay up until one o'clock in the morning. Of course we still have to get up at the usual time the next day, but we don't object. We depend on the spiritual nourishment from the broadcasts.

"My father, who lives with us, spends all his spare hours experimenting with the antenna trying to improve reception. When the programs come on, my father leans into the radio as if he is in the same room with those speaking. My boy Misha sits by the hour at the short-wave radio tuning the dial to discover if there are other Christian broadcasts we are missing. My daughter Nadia considers the Christian broadcaster part of our family. She wrote to Aunt Tania, who tells children Bible stories, but it is doubtful that her letter ever got past the censor."

Despite Soviet censorship, the missionary radio stations have received several thousand letters from the U.S.S.R. Many Christians in Barnaul wrote to express their gratitude—and often to ask for literature. One listener, fearing confiscation, wrote to station FEBC in the Philippine Islands: "Please send me a homiletics book and works of expositors of the Gospel. We are praying that the foxes and rats will not steal this literature enroute. . . ."

Besides listening to the broadcasts themselves, believers in Barnaul frequently invited non-Christians to listen and used these opportunities to witness about Christ. One morning a foreman at the factory where Petr T. worked said, "I heard a radio program last night about God. Do you think the speaker was telling the truth?" Petr encouraged his foreman to listen again and offered, "Each day we can discuss what you hear."

One Christian, Innokentii M., used his radio as a preacher in the huge apartment building where he lived. "It was during the 24th Communist Party Congress," Innokentii recalls. "The authorities had cut back on jamming, as they customarily did when they knew that foreign delegates would be visiting our country. The Gospel broadcasts came through the clearest I'd ever heard them. I opened my doors and windows, and soon an eager crowd had gathered in the hall."

A few days later a Communist Party supervisor at the factory summoned Innokentii to his office. "I hear you're having church meetings at your apartment," he said with a frown.

"No," Innokenti replied, "we were just listening to our radio." He scribbled on a piece of paper. "Here—this is the number on the dial where you can find the station yourself."

In a city north of Barnaul, a judge was converted through the radio broadcasts. In another Siberian city, a former Russian army general who had known Lenin and fought with him in the 1917 Revolution became a Christian after listening to the broadcasts.

Barnaul believers were strengthened by the Gospel broadcasts in their own language. They appreciated programs on which the Bible was read at dictation speed. But they refused to relinquish the hope of having their own Bibles.

Persistently, they pled with their government to authorize more Bible printings. They reminded Soviet authorities about constitutional guarantees of freedom of the press.

In 1970 a surprising Novosti Press Agency article affirmed Soviet legal provision for printing religious literature:

> The constitution of the U.S.S.R. guarantees every citizen of the Soviet Union, both religious and nonreligious, freedom of the press. This fundamental law insures the freedom of the press by granting to religious citizens supplies of state paper stock, printing shops, and other necessary equipment and materials for publishing printed matter. Just as all other Soviet citizens, the followers of various religions exercise this right and publish the religious literature they need.[7]

Such articles seemed an audacious lie to believers in Barnaul, who had never been allowed to publish desperately needed Christian literature. Some had tried.

But that involved immense difficulty, since typewriters, mimeographing and duplicating machines, and even quantities of paper are virtually impossible to obtain in Russia. Private citizens who possess duplicating materials are in danger.

Some took the risk anyway. In a court indictment against a Christian from the Ukraine, the authorities reported confiscating the following: "Recipe for hecto-graphing, gelatin, glue, manganese, drawing paper, a press to bind books and magazines, and an article from the Soviet Magazine *Nauka i Zhizn* (Science and Life) with advice on binding magazines in home conditions."

Despite the danger of imprisonment, Christians from CCECB churches, including the one in Barnaul, regularly mimeographed literature and also protest documents that they wanted to circulate within their own country and to the West.

In 1965, *Bratskii Listok* (*Fraternal Leaflet*) appeared, a regular pamphlet with current news of persecution among widely scattered CCECB churches. Spiritual exhortation, devotional material, and urgent appeals for prayer accompanied the accounts.

As clandestinely as possible, CCECB members mimeographed this magazine, which came out about three times a year. Besides *Bratskii Listok,* other devotional material was circulated. The *Bulletin of the Council of Prisoners' Relatives* also began to appear in 1969, reproduced by the same laborious methods.

But whenever it was discovered, duplication of Christian literature was severely punished by Soviet authorities. On January 9, 1966, the police of the Railroad District seized copies of *Collection of Spiritual Poems for Children and Youth* from Petr Ivanovich Gibert. In February, 1967, the procurator of the Altai Territory instituted criminal proceedings against Gibert.

When he was fined 300 rubles and sentenced to three years in prison, the Barnaul Christians wrote indignant-ly:

It turns out that ancient Hebrew people three thousand years ago were in a better condition than we are now in the second half of the twentieth century. They transmitted by hand their geneologies and history of their life and culture, which all humanity now reads and studies with delight on the pages of the ancient memorial of writing, the Bible. They at least were not subjected to criminal proceedings for their copying. And we, like the ancient Jews, copy by hand that spiritual heritage which we would wish to transmit to our children, and for this we receive terms of imprisonment and monetary fines. . . .

In 1971 Baptist reformers announced the existence of their own printing agency called Khristianin ("The Christian"), and soon Bibles and other literature from this secret press began to appear. In their announcement the believers reminded the Soviet government to print Bibles for them, or else to allow believers to establish their own printing press according to rights guaranteed in the constitution.

The Soviet government has assiduously tried to track down Khristianin. They have succeeded in seizing one of the presses and imprisoning some of the Christians involved. Other presses are still operating.

Russian believers do not dare reveal details of the printing press operation. A woman from Siberia whose husband helps bind Bibles says simply, "Those who are involved are in voluntary imprisonment. Often they work day and night in cellars, attics, and other concealed places. They must go weeks and sometimes months without seeing their families. They live in constant fear of discovery."

After the literature is printed, Christians still face the terrifying risk of distributing it, a risk that has also led to imprisonment for some.

But the thirst for Scripture compels the Christians to persevere. In Barnaul, the believers tell the story of two *dedushki* (grandfathers) from the church who helped distribute the literature. One of the old men carrying two heavy suitcases bulging with Bibles slipped on ice and twisted his ankle. He stood up, lifted the suitcases, and said to his companion, "Ah, well . . . the Scriptures say that 'we must through much tribulation enter into the kingdom of God!' "

1. Walter Sawatsky, "Bible Work in Eastern Europe Since 1945 (Part 2)" *Religion in Communist Lands,* Vol. 3, No. 6, October-November-December, 1975, p. 11.

2. L. Serdobolskaia, "Under Cover of the Gospel," *Leningradskaia Pravda,* October 12, 1967. (Translated in *Religion in Communist Dominated Areas,* Vol. VII, Nos. 19-20, October 15/30, 1968, pp. 186-188.)

3. N. Aminov, "Atheist at the Microphone—A Light Against Darkness," *Pravda Vostoka,* January 25, 1972. (Translated in *Religion in Communist Dominated Areas,* Vol. XII, Nos. 4-6, April-May-June, 1973, p. 77.)

4. Vladimir A. Kuroedov, "Firebrands," *Izvestiia,* October 18, 1969. (Translated in *Religion in Communist Dominated Areas,* Vol. X, Nos. 3-6, February-March, 1971, p. 33.)

5. A. Belov and A. Shilkin, "Diversionary Tactics over the Airwaves," *Nauka i Religiia,* No. 5, 1970, p. 46. (Translated in *Religion in Communist Dominated Areas,* Vol. IX, Nos. 1-2, January, 1970, p. 8.)

6. From Radio Moscow's domestic service in Russia, April 18, 1972. (Translated in *Religion in Communist Dominated Areas,* Vol. XI, Nos. 4-6, April-May-June, 1972, p. 55.)

7. Fedor Savin, "Religious Publications in the Soviet Union," Novosti Press Agency, 1970. (Translated in *Religion in Communist Dominated Areas,* Vol. XI, Nos. 4-6, April-May-June, 1972, p. 72.)

14

"Human Rights"

WITH NOBLE INTENTIONS the United Nations designated 1968 as the International Year of Human Rights. During this year the nations of the world reaffirmed the 1948 U.N. Declaration of Human Rights, from which the following clauses are taken:

Article 5
No one shall be subjected to torture or to cruel, inhuman or degrading treatment or punishment.

Article 10
Everyone is entitled in full equality to a fair and public hearing by an independent and impartial tribunal, in the determination of his rights and obligations and of any criminal charge against him.

Article 12
No one shall be subjected to arbitrary interference with his privacy, family, home, or correspondence, nor to attacks upon his honor and reputation. Everyone has the right to the protection of the law against such interference or attacks.

Article 13, Section 2
Everyone has the right to leave any country, including his own, and to return to his country.

Article 18
Everyone has the right to freedom of thought, conscience, and religion; this right includes freedom to change his religion or belief, and freedom, either alone or in community with others, and in public or private, to manifest his religion or belief in teaching, practice, worship and observance.

Article 20, Section 1
Everyone has the right to freedom of peaceful assembly and association.

The U.S.S.R. was one of the first nations to subscribe to this declaration in 1948, and in 1968 the Soviets endorsed it once again.

In Barnaul, the Soviet Union's public pronouncements and local actions did not coincide. A new wave of searches, disruptions, fines, and arrests preceded Human Rights Year in Barnaul. During February and March, 1967, the authorities interrogated several of the Christian children and even asked them to write denunciations of their own parents. An open letter records the interrogations of Vova Budimir, Sasha Airikh, Vova Airikh, Sasha Shtertser, and Misha Bogomiachikov, all children from the church.

Police also persisted in searching believers' homes and confiscating Christian literature and documents. They then used the literature as evidence to charge believers under the clause in Article 142 forbidding "the preparation for the purpose of mass distribution of petitions, letters, leaflets, and other documents which call for infringement of the laws concerning religious cults."

On April 18-22, 1967, Yakov Bil, Yakov Pauls, Petr

Gibert, Aron Dik, Lidiia Neifeld, Vatslava Lovkaites (an invalid woman), and Luiza Shtertser (at the time six months pregnant) were tried in the Railroad Workers' Club after being forced to sign statements promising not to depart from the city. While several hundred people in the courtroom observed, authorities accused the Christians under the amended Article 142 for activities dating from 1960—although the article was only a year old at the time.

Yakov Bil and Petr Gibert were each sentenced to three years general regime, and Gibert was also fined three hundred rubles for possession of religious literature. Yakov Pauls was sentenced to two years general regime. The other four were fined a twenty-five percent deduction of wages for one year. Also, Zelma Gauf was fined fifty rubles.

That September, Yurii Mikhalkov formally petitioned the Soviet government to lift the surveillance of Christians by the KGB, but he received no reply. The authorities' only response was to intensify persecution against the Barnaul believers.

As Human Rights Year began, they knew they were in a supernatural struggle. "We at present live with the feeling of being in some kind of wartime and occupied territory," they wrote. Sixty-four CCECB believers from across Russia went to prison in 1968. By the end of the year, more than two hundred CCECB members were in jail.

On June 23, 1968, Kornei Korneevich Kreker, a Christian visiting Barnaul from Mezhdurechensk, was arrested as he walked with his wife along Severozapadnaia Street. On September 13, 1968, Vatslava Osipovna Lovkaites, the invalid, was again arrested in Barnaul. Lidiia Andreevna Neifeld was arrested that same evening.

Police accused both women of "corrupting children with Christian teaching."

Members of the Christian Council of Prisoners' Relatives (CPR) wrote to U Thant, secretary general of the United Nations, in August to complain that the Soviet authorities had blatantly ignored their affirmation of human rights in dealing with the CCECB churches in Russia. The council members expressed their gratitude for the declaration, but as Lidiia Vins pointed out in the letter, the Christians could not help wondering whether it also applied to them:

> . . . Last year we sent you detailed letters about persecutions of evangelical Christians and Baptist believers who live within the territory of the U.S.S.R. Until now we have received no answer.
>
> It was the will of the Lord that the United Nations should declare the year 1968 as the International Year of Human Rights for the celebration of the twentieth anniversary of the General Declaration of Human Rights. As far as we know, every country must adapt its legislation to agree with this declaration and warrant personal freedom—religious freedom included. Now the eighth month of 1968 is approaching its end, but at the same time the number of prisoners who go to jail because they preach the Word of God has not decreased and their conditions in the prisons have not changed. Police fill the prisons with other Christians to replace those who finish their terms of punishment. During the past year another thirty were added to the list of prisoners from CCECB churches. Again this means that hundreds of children have been made orphans.
>
> For us the International Year of Human Rights is passing with new reinforced persecution. Peaceful worship services are dispersed; believers who participate are fined and sentenced to fifteen days without food; children are removed from Christian parents because they are brought up with

religious instruction; and homes are searched and spiritual literature confiscated. We cannot describe our sufferings.

We beg you to communicate to us the result of our petition to you, and also whether the agreement of human rights is also valid for us.

As 1969 approached, believers in Barnaul had little reason to feel that their government's siege against them had lifted. The CPR's plea to U Thant was unanswered. Rampantly the searches, interrogations, fines and even arrests continued. Now even children were interrogated more frequently.

Evald Gauf, owner of the prayer house which police destroyed in 1966, was again hounded in 1969. On September 23, citizens in civilian clothing arrived in an unmarked Volga car and coerced Gauf to go with them to the police station. Next, at the Railroad Regional Executive Committee, he had to face the notorious Comrade Gorbatenko, who since 1961 had been instrumental in planning persecution of believers in Barnaul.

After a special session, the Regional Executive Committee issued Decision Number 234: Gauf was to be sent to a raw materials factory to perform one year of "labor beneficial to society." Twenty percent of his wages would be deducted monthly for the benefit of the state, even though Gauf had a family to support.

But when the factory superintendent discovered Gauf was a believer, the superintendent refused him a job. Gauf was transferred to the Altai automotive plant, but here also officials hesitated to hire a believer, even though he had passed all examinations for an electrician's job. Finally, Gauf received a lower position there. Before they officially hired him, factory officials reprimanded Gauf for "idleness" during the time he had not been permitted to work.

Despite continuing harassments, the year 1969 some-how seemed slightly more encouraging to the Barnaul believers than the Year of Human Rights, which had promised so much but delivered so little. By this time the congregation had enlarged its ties with CCECB congregations across Russia. The church had also become increasingly active in the national Council of Prisoners' Relatives. In open letters they included accounts of persecution and other open letters from Christians in places outside Barnaul, such as Prokopevsk, Kasikovo, Pavlodar, Dubrava, Krivoi Rog, Lobzovka, and Omsk.

Barnaul Christians also organized jubilee meetings in 1969 to celebrate the release of Yakov Bil and Petr Gibert as well as other CCECB prisoners from congregations outside Barnaul.*

The same year, the Soviet government permitted the AUCECB to hold another national congress in Moscow. In his address, AUCECB President I. G. Ivanov said, "We are continually saying to our separated [CCECB] brothers: Let's work together; there were mistakes on our part as there also were on yours. Today we have listened to reports and we have seen how many mistakes there were on one or the other side. Therefore, we must come together and say: We were mistaken—some in one way, others in another, and now we wish to be in error no longer but to be together fulfilling the prayer of our Lord Jesus Christ, 'That they may all be one.' "

Such conciliatory communications did bring some un-registered Christians back to AUCECB churches. Au-

---

*Although set in remote Siberia, Barnaul served as a center for Christian reunions. Aida Skripnikova, a bold young woman from Leningrad who served four years in prison for her faith, was welcomed there. CCECB leaders Gennadii Kriuchkov and Georgii Vins, who had both suffered in prison several times, also visited Barnaul to encourage the believers.

thorities allowed a few CCECB congregations to register. And, as before, some Christians attended services at both registered AUCECB and unregistered CCECB churches. In some cities close fellowship existed between the two groups.

But even though leaders from both groups had negotiated during 1969 and agreed that church unity was vital, many Christians from CCECB churches felt wary about returning to the AUCECB. Many of the reformers still strongly distrusted some of the leading AUCECB officials, who they felt were willing to compromise their faith.

The hopes of the CCECB Christians revived in December, 1969, when they were finally given official permission to hold their first national congress. The reformers earnestly hoped this meant that the government was at last willing to legally recognize CCECB congregations. Perhaps at last they would be allowed to register without relinquishing the reforms they had suffered to gain.

On December 6, 1969, one hundred twenty preachers from CCECB churches across Russia gathered in the city of Tula, 150 kilometers south of Moscow. They met in the home of N. I. Vladykin, 14 Krasnodontsy Street. During the congress, CCECB council members were chosen, including Dmitrii Miniakov from Barnaul, who was reelected even though he was at that moment in prison. Shortly afterward, the council asked Soviet authorities to allow eight members of the CCECB to work as full-time ministers of the church. The reformers hoped that at last the days of hiding were over for evangelists.

But their high hopes were short-lived. Although at this time CCECB congregations across Russia were submitting requests for registration, in most instances this information was used only to plan new campaigns of repression. The 120 CCECB leaders who thought they had received government permission to meet freely in Tula found themselves treated like fugitives. Some were arrested. The secretary of the CCECB council, Georgii Vins, was charged with parasitism—being unemployed. Authorities confiscated the house in Tula where the council had met, and owner Vladykin was sentenced to a year of forced labor.

Meanwhile, the Barnaul congregation had been meeting at Aleksandr Shtertser's house on 63 Voleibolnaia Drive since the destruction of Gauf's house four years earlier. To make more room for the meetings, Shtertser removed the inner walls of his house, reserving only one small bedroom. The Shtertsers at first balanced boards across wooden logs for benches. Later some of the deacons built simple wooden benches, which the Shtertsers pushed to one side of the room during the day to make more living space.

The police persistently tried to dislodge the determined believers from their new meeting place. On December 17, 1969, a local communist official summoned Shtertser to the Railroad Club. The next day the believers sent protest telegrams to the U.S.S.R. Supreme Court and the United Nations. They reminded the authorities that their first prayer house had been destroyed by order of the communist officials. "Now if the authorities are going to destroy this home, there is nothing left but to destroy us together with the home by bulldozer!" the Christians stated.

In 1970 the Barnaul believers applied once again to the Altai Regional Executive Committee for legal permission to register their prayer house on Voleibonaia Drive as a church:

179

For the combined fulfilling of our religious require-
ments, we the citizens, numbering 250 people, under the
direction of the Council of Churches of the Evangelical
Christians-Baptists (CCECB) of the U.S.S.R., decided to
register our church of Evangelical Christians-Baptists which
has been active since 1961. The areas of the activity of our
church will be developed according to the discretion of our
church. We ask that our group be registered under the
name of the Barnaul Church of the Evangelical
Christians-Baptists whose address is Voleibolnaia Drive,
Number 63, which will be temporary until we are granted a
permanent location.

The Barnaul congregation received no reply until
January, 1971. Then came a letter from their long-time
acquaintance, Comrade Gorbatenko, now president of
the Railroad Regional Executive Committee. He severely
warned them not to hold meetings, since they "lacked
registration." In March the committee dispatched deputies to visit believers' homes. The deputies read solemnly from a letter with a stamp and seal that accused the
believers of "not registering."

During 1970, harassment of Barnaul believers was not
just confined to meetings they conducted in their own
town in the house on Voleibolnaia Drive. Christians from
Barnaul also traveled to Troitskoe, Bolshaia Rechka,
Ozero Krasilovo, Pavlovsk, and Shumanovka to visit
other churches. In each of these cities they were harried
by the police and in some instances beaten and detained
in the police station.

On October 18, 1970, some members of the Barnaul
church orchestra traveled to a harvest festival at the
church in Kulunda, where Nikolai Khmara had lived.
During the service, some of the same police who had
arrested Khmara appeared at the meeting and beat sev-

eral of the believers. The police confiscated several musical instruments and hauled some of the Christians to the police station.

On that same Sunday in Barnaul, other members of the unregistered congregation had gathered at Shterster's house to celebrate Communion. A police delegation in uniform headed by the district policeman, Fedor Markovich Stepanov, stormed into the house with a complaint supposedly submitted by the neighborhood. The statement said that the Christians "were disturbing neighbors who worked the night shift and had to sleep during the day." Further, the neighbors complained that the Christians were "enticing minors into their religious meetings by serving wine at Communion." Because he had opened his home for this church service, the authorities deducted fifty rubles from Aleksandr Shterster's pension.

A few days before Easter, 1971, Evald Gauf traveled to the village of Bolshaia Rechka Station to celebrate Communion with the believers there. Police came to the home where Gauf was staying and arrested him. Later they took him to Biisk, where they held him in custody. After twenty-two days, Gauf refused to eat. On the thirty-first day, he was released.

The Barnaul believers wearily looked back to 1961 when their house meetings had begun. They had undergone five court trials, which sent nine of their members to prisons and camps. They had experienced twenty-six searches with fines totaling two thousand rubles. Their prayer house, valued at about six thousand rubles, had been destroyed.

After nearly a decade of struggle, many believers in

Barnaul felt that the dark cloud of persecution might never lift. But clinging to God all the more, they refused to despair. They met more often to pray and share strength from the Bible. The Scriptures became their daily guide and sustenance. In an open letter they wrote:

That's how it always is with holy truth,
For men love sinful darkness more than light.
They quench our campfires burning in the night,
And fill their prisons with men who love truth.

For we ought to say, "If the Lord will,
We shall live, and do this, or that." (James 4:15)

15

Acts 12 Revisited

AFTER HIS STRICT-REGIME prison term in the early sixties, Dmitrii Miniakov, the much-loved presbyter of the Barnaul congregation, was in failing health. On August 25, 1967, he was arrested for the second time. At a show trial in the club of the sheepskin factory on February 14, 1968, he was sentenced to three years of strict regime and soon shipped to prison. His major "offense": participating in the group that had questioned the delay of registration for Gauf's house back in 1965.

Miniakov's wife Antonina begged local prison officials for permission to bring her husband a Bible, but they refused. She then wrote to the Presidium of the Supreme Soviet of the U.S.S.R. on July 8, asking them to forward a Bible to her imprisoned husband.

She reminded the authorities of the U.N. charter resolutions on maintaining penitentiaries. "These resolutions protect the prisoners' right to have Bibles, prayer books, and to take the Lord's Supper," she wrote. She pleaded with Moscow officials to heed the charter which they had openly endorsed.

On August 1, Antonina received an answer from the chief administrator of places of confinement of the

U.S.S.R. He wrote, "In corrective institutions and places of deprivation of freedom in our country, it is permitted to use only literature printed by Soviet state publishing houses. Since Bibles have never been published by state publishing houses during the years of Soviet rule, reading of the Bible in prisons is forbidden." He thus conveniently ignored the Bibles printed under Soviet authorization, including 20,000 copies during that year alone.

But Antonina did not give up. She sent a second request to the Presidium pleading again that her husband be allowed the consolation of a Bible. This time the Presidium replied sharply that such questions were "not within its jurisdiction."

For the next two years, Dmitrii suffered in prison with severe asthma. Officials eventually transferred him to the prison hospital.

Concerned about his condition, Antonina wrote to the Council of Prisoners' Relatives on April 15, 1970, asking them to pray earnestly for her husband.

She reported that Miniakov had suffered another asthma attack on January 15, 1970. He was not given the medicine prescribed by his doctor, but instead given other medicine that did not help him. On January 29 he received ten injections of a medicine for which only two injections had been prescribed. "This had a disastrous effect on Dmitrii's heart," Antonina recorded. "From January 15th until now my husband has been suffering from oxygen starvation and has been lying on an oxygen pillow. I am very worried in case he should be moved. I don't know how he would stand up to another journey."

On Tuesday, August 25, 1970, Dmitrii Miniakov's prison term ended. With great joy, Antonina Miniakov and several friends and relatives went to the prison to meet her husband. Dmitrii was scheduled to be released at three that afternoon, but the anxious Christians gathered early (see photo section).

At noon a man strode out of the prison gate, walked past the waiting Christians, and sped away in a Volga. Terror-stricken, the Christians recognized the man—a KGB agent who had been instrumental in directing the court proceedings against Miniakov. This same official had led the disruption of a harvest festival meeting at the home of G. I. Mantai in 1963. He had also participated in detaining Evald Gustavovich Gauf during 1966 and 1967.

A tremor of fear tore through Antonina. Why was the agent there? Would he prevent her husband's release?

When Dmitrii finally walked through the prison gates that afternoon, Antonina wept with relief.

The following Sunday, the Barnaul CCECB church planned a jubilant thanksgiving service to celebrate the return of their presbyter. A week earlier they had sent a petition to Comrade I. I. Molchaninov, chairman of the Altai Regional Executive Committee, requesting permission for a place to hold their meeting, but had received no answer.

Since none of the believers lived in a house large enough to hold all who wanted to attend, the church decided to meet in the yard of Artur Vladimirovich Pritskau, a member who lived at 37 Omsk Street.

That Sunday the morning skies were gray and foreboding. When the believers arrived, they discovered the district policeman, Fedor Markovich Stepanov, standing at Pritskau's gates. Other police patrolled the yard shouting into a megaphone, "Disperse immediately!" By the time the meeting began, almost as many police as Christians had assembled.

A few blocks from Pritskau's house, the police had

parked buses, which they planned to use to carry away the Christians. But they could not navigate the buses down the mud road bordering Pritskau's house.

Nevertheless, the police drove eight of the Christian men to the Railroad Regional Executive Committee building and held them for six hours. Kondrat Solomonovich Rudi, one of the eight, boldly demanded that the police prepare a protocol stating the reason for the detention. At four that afternoon the official in charge shooed the men from his office with the words, "Get out of here—while you still can!"

By any description, Dmitrii Miniakov's welcome meeting had been tumultuous. But the presbyter, worn and now sick from tuberculosis, was thankful just to be home again with Antonina and their five children. And, although KGB officials had strictly warned him not to, Miniakov soon returned to his responsibilities in the Barnaul church.

But Miniakov's freedom would last only 14 months.

During the fall of 1971, members of the Railroad Executive Committee's newly elected, magnificently titled Commission for the Supervision of the Observation of Soviet Legislation Concerning Religious Cults started to visit the unregistered church meetings. In September, Nadezhda Ivanovna Antonova, chairwoman of the commission, attended the house meeting.

Later that month five Christian leaders received summonses to appear at the commission: A. A. Shtertser, P. B. Drizner, Vladimir Firsov, Evald Gauf—and Dmitrii Miniakov. All were accused of arranging the worship service of September 11, even though Miniakov had not conducted the service.

On November 19, the presbyter was arrested for the third time and placed under guard at the order of the

Altai territorial procurator. On the same day searches were conducted in his apartment and several others'.

Weak and dying, Dmitrii was hauled off once again to prison. He refused to eat. He told the police, "First I will fast and pray one week for our church, then one week for my family, then . . . ."

"But you have five children, Dmitrii Vasilevich," the police argued. "You must think of your family. You cannot afford to starve yourself to death."

Ten days passed and Miniakov refused food. Soldiers were summoned to try to force-feed him. One soldier pinned his arms to the back of the chair. Another bent Miniakov's head backward until his bones cracked and he lost consciousness. After this the soldiers shoved a stick into Miniakov's mouth, but spasms in his throat made their efforts futile. All of this happened under the supervision and direction of the hospital doctor in the Barnaul prison investigation isolation room 17/1, according to a document from the Barnaul congregation.

During Miniakov's fast at the prison, his wife Antonina and the other Christians kept vigil with him in prayer and fasting. One of the deacons vividly recalls those days. "We felt that our experience was similar to the church of Acts. In their persecutions they prayed, and miracles happened. We prayed for the release of our brother Dmitrii—which we knew would take a miracle.

"On Wednesday, December 1, our church had gathered in a home to pray for Dmitrii. While his name was on our lips, a knock sounded on the door. A messenger told us, 'Your friend Dmitrii is now in the city hospital. Procurator Krasnoirtsev has transferred him from the prison.' We felt like the Christians in Acts who could not believe that Peter had been released from prison!

"Antonina and several of us immediately rushed to the hospital. Even if we were not allowed in his room, we knew it was important that other witnesses from our church be present in case the authorities harassed Antonina.

"The police would not allow us into the hospital, but they did admit that our brother Dmitrii was inside. The next morning Antonina and some of us returned. The procurator was waiting for us. 'You can take him home,' he said crossly. But first he made Brother Dmitrii, so weak he could barely write, sign a guarantee he would not leave the city.

"We all knew that our brother could have been sentenced for as long as five years—even though he was innocent. He was released in less than a month. God had performed a miracle."

16

The Passport Affair

TO THE BARNAUL BELIEVERS, Dmitrii Miniakov's third arrest had been a terrible injustice. But even after his early release, rumors circulated that the police were plotting new arrests.

For ten years the Barnaul Christians had continuously pled through every legal channel for a stop to religious persecution. They had conscientiously conducted themselves as hard-working Soviet citizens. They had tried to obey the laws of their land, and petitioned their government likewise to heed constitutional guarantees of religious freedom.

The brave band of believers had struggled valiantly, not just for themselves but on behalf of all Christians in Russia. Would their sufferings ever end? The monolithic Soviet government still seemed determined to eventually crush anyone they considered a hindrance to the "construction of communist society."

Night after night during the fall of 1971 the church leaders gathered quietly. They fasted, prayed, and asked God for direction.

After much searching, they knew what they should do. Christians from the unregistered church had not been

189

treated like Soviet citizens for eleven years. Therefore, it seemed only logical that they should return to the government their documents of citizenship—the internal passports which all Soviet citizens from age sixteen must carry at all times in order to travel within the country or obtain many other privileges. "A Soviet citizen without a passport is a citizen who doesn't exist," the folk saying went.

Rather than affording them privileges of citizenship, believers in Barnaul decided that their passports (listing such details as name, birthdate, nationality) had actually been used as a pretext for harassing and arresting them.

For example, on Wednesday, November 24, 1971, police arrived at the home of David Benovich Drizner. They pushed their way into the house and demanded to "check the passports of the homeowners."

The police spied a drum and some other musical instruments which they suspected the Drizners used in the church orchestra. "You're trying to start another church!" one of the policemen accused.

Drizner blocked the doorway into the rooms where the instruments stood neatly lined against the wall. Four police officers grabbed him, twisted his arms behind his back, and dragged him into the street. They shoved and bruised his pregnant wife Yelena while their five children screamed in terror. Taking six instruments, the police left with the threat, "Others besides Miniakov are going to be sentenced to jail."

After much consideration the Barnaul Christians wrote President Podgorny a letter they planned to deliver personally to Moscow: "We prefer not to have passports or military service cards, which give the police an excuse for beating, maltreating, or bringing us to court."

In a later open letter, the believers explained:

> The church decided to . . . turn in passports and military service cards . . . since long ago we had already been deprived of our civil rights. Our condition has been worse than that of Negroes or any other oppressed people. We are deprived even of the possibility of praying and worshiping the Creator and Ruler of the world. Spiritual oppression is more agonizing than physical oppression, and we are suffering both.

"We want to enjoy the rights of free citizens in real life and not simply possess the documentary certification of a citizen—a passport," they wrote in another letter.

With great caution, they laid plans to return their documents to the authorities in Moscow. They knew their unprecedented plan would be severely punished if it were discovered. But they hoped that the unheard-of surrender of passports would shock the authorities into listening at last.

If the hundreds of protest documents they had mailed before had never reached their destination, there seemed little prospect that the passports and accompanying letter of explanation would ever arrive intact at the Kremlin. Thus, two men and two women were inconspicuously chosen to gather the passports and deliver them by hand to Moscow.

With great secrecy the committee collected 130 personal documents from among the congregation. Then they circulated a letter to members of the Presidium which each of the passport holders signed, stating that the passports were surrendered voluntarily to protest against persecution of Christians.

As a precaution, the four Christians also copied each of the passports while someone stood sentry, watching for the police. The committee had kept details of their plan from the rest of the congregation—where the passports were kept and who would carry them finally to Moscow. But despite all their precautions, they could not help worrying as they worked night after night compiling the passports and laboriously photographing each one: Had a Judas somehow overheard their plans?

On the day in November, 1971, that the committee flew to Moscow, their families accompanied them to the stop where they planned to catch the bus for the Barnaul airport. As they neared the bus stop by the railroad station, a procession of yellow and blue *militsiia* cars approached. The Christians stood petrified. After all their struggle and sacrifice, were they to be halted at the last moment?

But the police cars, apparently on another errand, slowly passed by.

The Christians' fears did not subside even after they arrived in Moscow. But on the morning set for delivering the passports, a calm certainty of God's purpose compassed the four.

They set off for the Kremlin clutching the passports in a small package. They passed tourists gathered by the tsar bell and cannon, hurried by a huge, hunched statue of Lenin, and stood before the stately Presidium building. One of them recalls, "With every step toward the Kremlin we thought of our brothers and sisters back in Barnaul praying—and we felt strengthened." As they approached the Presidium, with its red hammer and sickle flag swirling in the wind, the four Christians decided that the two women would wait outside to watch—and flee if the men were caught inside.

In the Presidium offices, a policeman guarded the admissions window at which a woman receptionist stood.

"What do you want?" he asked as he surveyed the two Christians.

But before they could reply, the policeman, who apparently thought he heard footsteps on the stairs, dashed toward the noise calling, "Who's there?"

The Christian turned quickly to the receptionist. "Will you please give these important papers to the authorities for me?" he asked, politely handing her the package. She took the package and turned from her desk to examine it. The Christians hurried from the building, mingled rapidly with passersby, and walked through Trinity Gate out of the Kremlin. They flew out of Moscow on the next plane home without the authorities, or even most of the believers in Barnaul, ever knowing who the messengers had been.

One of the men recalls solemnly, "If God had not protected us, we surely would have been arrested and would probably be sitting in prison today."

As the Christians had predicted, the Moscow authorities were shocked. They quickly relayed word to Barnaul. Since the local officials did not know the identity of the messengers, they summoned several leaders from the unregistered congregation. "Who delivered these to Moscow?" they demanded furiously. Most of the Christians could reply that they honestly did not know.

"Never before in the history of the Soviet Union has such a thing happened," one of the chief officials sputtered in anger mingled with bewilderment. "All of Moscow is talking about this. The whole country—the whole world will know about it. You must take back your passports immediately before word of your outrageous actions spreads even further. Don't you fools know it is a privilege to be a Soviet citizen?" he shouted.

But the Christians would not be badgered. "You forced us into this," they said. "If you had not persecuted us for eleven years, we obviously would not have given up our citizenship."

"But why didn't you come to us first before you went to Moscow?"

The Christians smiled ruefully. "We have lost track of the many times we tried to ask you for help," one of the deacons said. "Now it is too late."

In the following months the local authorities called on the Barnaul Christians, cajoling and finally demanding that the believers take back their passports. "Not until we are treated like real Soviet citizens" was the reply.

The courage of some other CCECB churches in the Soviet Union was bolstered by the action. They told their authorities, "If you do not stop treating us illegally, we will turn in our passports like the Christians in Barnaul did!"

The bold protest drew national and even some international attention to the plight of believers in Barnaul. It did not persuade the authorities, however, to grant civil rights to Christians in their city. Barnaul police continued to disrupt meetings, conduct searches, and arrest believers.

On March 13, 1972, Yurii Mikhalkov, the young engineer who had already spent two grueling terms in prison, was arrested again by authorities determined to stop the flow of documents from his pen. For eleven days Mikhalkov fasted. After being forcibly fed on the twelfth day, he took food. By this time the sturdy prisoner, only thirty-five years old, was sick and suffering. Strict-regime prison and constant struggle with authorities had wrecked his health. His parents, Ivan Andreevich and

Maria Ilinichna, pled for his trial to be postponed. But their petition was rejected.

Later, forty-two of the Christians wrote to the United Nations as well as the general secretary of the Communist Party Central Committee to describe Yurii's blatantly unjust trial:

This is not the first trial of a believer to take place in our town. We are already accustomed to the deceptive behavior of the investigators and public prosecutors in announcing, for the benefit of the parents and relations, that a trial will take place in one spot, while in fact it is being held somewhere totally different. All this is done to fill the courtroom with especially chosen people and to prevent believers from attending the trial.

This very thing happened on March 31 when it was announced that Yurii Mikhalkov's trial would take place in the area court building. But in fact all the people were gathered at the opposite end of the town in the Ovchina Club, a fur factory. By the time the believers had arrived at the Ovchina Club, the room was full and they were not allowed to the front but forced to take seats in the back rows.

This served yet another purpose. Out of all the people present, the photographers occupied themselves only with the condemned and the group of believers gathered at the back of the room. At the direction of persons in plain clothes they came right up to the believers, turned a bright, blinding light on them, and photographed them. This was done only to the believers in order to portray a distorted picture of them on television.

The fact that the believers are tried without having broken any law or committed any offense is shameful enough. But the behavior of the court and legal proceedings on March 31, when Yurii Mikhalkov was brought in with a reinforced guard of armed soldiers, *militsiia*, and a dog was even more shameful. Without witnesses or any proof of his guilt, he was sentenced to three years (under severe regime).

Our brother was found guilty under two articles—Article 142 and Article 190 of the penal code of the RSFSR.

The verdict was based on certain isolated phrases taken from the fourth and fifth open letters sent by the church in Barnaul to the government. In the open letters, we believers set out in detail the evidence of oppression and persecution of believers in our country. However, the court ignored these questions and dealt only with the isolated phrase— "concerning the course our government has taken to liquidate believers physically." They did not connect the phrase with facts demonstrating the real situation for believers.

The court decided that this phrase alone constituted enough evidence to convict our brother, Yurii Mikhalkov, under two articles—"slander of Soviet reality" and "calling for the breaking of the law concerning religious sects by means of appeals and writings."

But whatever phrases or extracts they might take from the letters, this material could not serve to convict Brother Mikhalkov, since the open letters were sent by the entire church—in other words, by all the believers. And they did not contain slander but actual facts from which it is impossible to escape either in this world or eternity.

The day after the trial, Yurii Mikhalkov was flown 125 miles north to Novosibirsk, placed in a condemned cell (a prison within a prison) for three months, and interrogated daily—sometimes for hours at a time. Then he was put in a punishment "refrigerator" cell for five days while his strength slowly slipped away. Soon, he started to cough blood from his lungs.

That summer, Yurii was transferred from Novosibirsk to a labor camp. His parents tried to visit the camp but were turned away harshly with the news that their son was "subject to special control." The camp commandant added, "We shall keep the pressure on, short of taking off his head."

In a letter dated August 20, 1972, Yurii's parents wrote from Barnaul to President Podgorny in Moscow to protest the cruel treatment of their son, which withheld even the comfort of a Bible:

> The question inevitably arises—are not these assaults a direct attempt on our son's life? In camp he has more than once asked to be allowed to have a New Testament. To his most recent request the prison commandant replied, "In state institutions, permitted literature is provided for you to read. Gospels are not attainable from libraries or book shelves."
>
> Can we as parents keep silent? Can our voices keep from crying out in defense of our son when we know the oppression he is undergoing? . . . We would also remind you that our son has not been able to receive letters nor write to us although he is guaranteed the right of two letters a month. . . . We ask you to listen to the cry of parents and to investigate our complaint—to put a halt to the humiliation and physical violence. The Lord will surely bless you for bringing justice in this matter.

The aging parents tried to console each other. Surely the authorities would finally pity their sick son, who had already spent so many years of his youth in prisons. But Mariia's hopes shriveled when she recalled a letter she had received from a prison commandant during Yurii's second term. Sadly she read it once again.

> In reply to your letter I inform you that your son Yurii Ivanovich Mikhalkov is in a place of confinement and is receiving all kinds of educational influence in order to turn him into a person useful for our socialist society and not for your circle of worshipers. Therefore all your prayer letters with quotations from church books are withheld and will be given to him on the day of his liberation.

As the educator of your son, I have a request for you as his mother and all your fellow believers. Do not write letters to him about church matters. He will not receive them and will be punished for them.

Your son had the highest education. And you as his mother succeeded in dragging him into a swamp from which he has gone into confinement for the second time. This should concern you and make you influence him to go the right way. But you are only dragging him further into the swamp.

All who are in confinement are limited in their actions, and their correspondence is subject to examination. Those letters which have a bad influence on the prisoner's education are confiscated. Thus, not all letters are given to your son.

For violation of the established regime, your son is deprived of food parcels. Until he has begun to reform—i. e., breaks with the circle of worshipers—he will not receive the monthly parcels, but instead will receive only one parcel every two months.

Therefore, my request to you is to help me liberate Yurii earlier by educating him to take his place in our socialist society and not in your narrow circle of worshipers. Then he may live together with his family and not separate from them. You, as his mother, ought to take all measures and means to educate Yurii so that he may not be "Yurii, martyr" but "Yurii Ivanovich, industrial engineer."

Regarding your request for a personal meeting, it depends upon you and your fellow believers. In May this year it may be granted to him—but not more than two days.

—Commandant of the Second Detachment
    Vinniakov

Vinniakov's earlier letter seemed to Yurii Mikhalkov's parents disheartening evidence that their son might be sealed in Soviet prisons forever. But they knew that Yurii would never break from his faith.

17

The Final Blow

AFTER ELEVEN YEARS of persecution, the Soviet government had not been able to break the adult Christians of Barnaul. Thus, in 1971 a sinister campaign was launched against the Christian schoolchildren.

But the attack was not new. It had been building for a long time.

In May, 1967, Antonina Miniakova, wife of the presbyter, had written to Leonid Brezhnev, general secretary of the Communist Party.

As the mother of five children, I am disturbed by the illegal actions of organs of the government with regard to our children. Without the knowledge of my husband and me, my children, who are attending School Number 54 in Barnaul, were called into separate offices by agents of the KGB and the procurator and interrogated for hours. One can imagine the state children are in when they are away from their parents and surrounded by investigators. If such interrogations have an impact on adults, they affect the health of our children even more.

I am stating the facts: In March, 1967, Detective Rylov of the regional procurator's office conducted an hour-long interrogation of my son Vova, born in 1958, a pupil in the second grade in School 54 in Barnaul.

On the morning of April 12, 1967, six agents of the KGB and the procurator's office searched our home, frightening the children. That same day Lena, born in 1954, was called right out of class by her teacher, Nadezhda Sergeevna. She was taken to the teachers' room, where a teacher from the department of atheism, Valentina Aleksandrovna Arzhevikina, was waiting for her. After a prolonged conversation led by Arzhevikina in the presence of three students, my daughter Lena came home seriously disturbed and barely slept the entire night because of a headache. On the next day, Lena did poorly in her lessons, could not even concentrate, left class three times in poor condition, and finally went to the school doctor.

On April 25 Lena became severely ill and stayed in bed with a high temperature. On that same day agents of the *militsiia* drove up and took me with my nursing infant to the procurator's office, while the four children were left at home crying and in a state of fright. After taking me to the procurator's office, Detective Bariuchkov began to ask me whether I knew any believers in Alma-Ata and whether I had had any correspondence with them.

I was disturbed at all these actions by the procurator's office and the *militsiia*. When I came home and found my children crying uncontrollably, I was struck with horror at all the lawlessness which is committed against us believers—not by some hooligans or brigands—but by those who look after order and by representatives of local government.

When will these torments against us stop? When will pedagogues of atheism stop deriding our children? If this continues any longer, we will be forced to keep our children from going to school.

Antonina Miniakova

Many other Christian mothers found the persecution of innocent children unconscionable. Two years after Antonina wrote to Brezhnev, Christian mothers from across Russia compiled a detailed document pleading that persecution against Christian children be stopped—that legislation which the U.S.S.R. had enacted or subscribed to protecting the rights of children be heeded. This protest, dated March, 1969, was courageously signed by 1,453 Christian mothers:

> As peaceful citizens of our country, we work and live quietly without harming others. . . . "All human beings are born free and alike in worth and rights"—thus runs one of the articles of the Declaration of Human Rights that you have agreed upon. It is valid both for you and for us. You, like ourselves, were once rocked in the cradle by a mother. How much love was included in the cradle songs they sang when we rested in their bosom! Your mothers wished you happiness in life. We also wish our children the same thing.

After citing cruel persecutions against their children, the Christian mothers pled:

> Be merciful . . . the word *mother* cannot be killed in a child's heart, and no atheistic rattles can console their sorrow. Who can fathom the despair of a child's soul when it is torn from its mother's hand? It is terrible to imagine that all this is happening now, and not in the days the woman author Harriet Beecher Stowe writes about in her book *Uncle Tom's Cabin,* where the child Harry was sold as a slave. All this happens while you are "protecting" the UNICEF children's fund for the children who suffer under racial discrimination.
>
> We can frankly say that our children are well developed and disciplined. They are not impaired by vices. You'll

never find our children among the tens of thousands of juvenile delinquents in this country.

Your aim to deprive our children of their religious instruction is quite clear to us. It does not happen because you care about our children, but the aim is to prevent the growth of the church. But Jesus said, "I will build my church; and the gates of hell shall not prevail against it."

We mothers, whose love for our children is unlimited, cannot give them to you to be ruined. We cannot and will not keep quiet any longer. They are our children. We have given them life. We also will defend them with all our might, and we are in our proper rights to do so. No intelligent person can contest the rights of a mother. Even the animals defend their offspring at the risk of their own lives.

Problems for the Christian children in Barnaul often began on the first day of school. Most of the Christian families were large. Consequently, school teachers often recognized the Christian children. And often—in violation of Lenin's 1918 decree on the separation of church and state*—a child's religious affiliations were recorded in his documents. A Christian child's health records, for example, might contain the notation "Baptist."

Yurii C., age seven, came from a large family in the Barnaul congregation. On his first day of school, his teacher Nina Ivanova greeted him. "Ah, Yurii," she said, "I remember your brothers Sasha and Petia and your sisters Olia, Katia, and Ania. Good students—all of them. But they would not change," she mused. "And you, little Yurichka—are you going to tell me that you are a *veruiushchii*, too?

*The Decree on the Separation of Church and State of January 23, 1918, states in Article 3: "Each citizen may confess any religion or no religion at all. Loss of any rights as the result of the confession of a religion or absence of a religion shall be revoked. The mention in official papers of the religion of a citizen is not allowed."

"No matter what your parents say, I must insist you join the Octoberists!"

Yurii's parents were well acquainted with the system of atheistic clubs which all Soviet schoolchildren are expected to join: the Octoberists, ages seven to nine, who wear a pin with a red star and silhouette of Lenin as a boy; the Young Pioneers, ages nine to fourteen, who wear a red scarf; and the final achievement for a Soviet young person—the Komsomol (Communist Youth League), which may be joined at the age of fifteen or sixteen.

Children who do not choose to join the clubs are automatically barred from many advantages. Most extracurricular activities are held at the Pioneer Palaces. Communist youth club members may take art, music, drama lessons and enjoy many other cultural advantages at no cost. Most athletic activities are sponsored through the clubs, and any child who expects to attend a university or succeed in Russia's highly competitive climb for professional jobs must belong to the clubs.

Although children are not legally required to join, most Soviet teachers exert every pressure to make sure that their students do. "How can you object to your children joining the Octoberists?" Yurii's teacher argued with his parents. "They will become nephews of Lenin, and Lenin was a good man." When this didn't help, the teacher tried to coerce the child. "Just wear your Lenin pin when you're at school, Yurichka. Your parents will never know that you belong."

Yurii still refused to join. Then his teacher enlisted peer pressure to change the seven-year-old Christian. She told three ten-year-old Pioneers, "You stand at the door and don't allow anyone to enter class unless they are wearing their Lenin pin or red scarf."

In Russia, some Christian parents feel that their children can join without compromising their convictions. Yurii's father, however, felt that the clubs were "the first step toward atheism, because atheism is the foundation for all that the children study in these organizations. The children are taught that there are no spiritual values in life and that man is only a higher form of animal. Besides this, they are taught to regard Christians as enemies of Soviet society; they are even instructed how to inform on believers—including their own parents. Unfortunately, our children are taught many of these same lessons even in regular classroom sessions, but not so constantly as if they are enrolled in the communist clubs.

"Even though they didn't belong to communist clubs, our children were still forced to watch atheistic films—often about 'misguided Christians' who had finally found the right path 'back to atheism'! Our children knew that we didn't want them to see these films. The schoolteacher also knew. But frequently when the children asked to be dismissed from these films, the teacher locked the room and insisted they stay.

"Even though we parents objected to the communist clubs, we could not force our children to refuse to join. The decision had to be their own. In school our children were constantly encouraged to break away from their family's beliefs—to betray their own parents. Like all Soviet children, ours were taught to revere Pavlik Morozov, the Young Pioneer in the 1930s who was murdered by his relatives because he betrayed his parents to the Soviet authorities for trying to assist banished *kulaks* [prosperous peasant farmers]. In the Komsomol, new members were forced to 'take a stand of hatred against all religion.' Younger children were expected to write essays describing every aspect of their home life."

Yurii's parents raised a thorough defense against such

efforts. "We were forced to prepare our children from infancy to face persecution for their faith. In the evenings, we always discussed the problems of the school day with our children. They knew that their conduct had to be exemplary—even the tiniest slip of bad behavior would be used by the teacher to condemn all Christians. Every morning we prayed with the children before they left for school. On communist holidays, we knew that our children would confront problems because they didn't belong to the clubs, and we tried to prepare them spiritually.

"We repeated the stories of David, Moses, Daniel, Peter, Stephen, and other faithful Christians to them. We reminded them of the Christian aunts and uncles in Russia imprisoned for their faith. 'If you join the Octoberists and then the Young Pioneers, you will be standing in opposition to all that our aunts and uncles in prison believe and have suffered for,' we told them.

"Of course we never asked our children to make these decisions without their certainty that we were standing right behind them. Our children knew we would do anything for them and that our whole family was in the struggle together to stand for our faith.

"Children were usually inducted into the communist clubs around November 7—Revolution Day. For several days before this time my wife and I prayed and fasted, asking God to strengthen our children for the difficulties we knew would come.

"One day my daughter Katia ran home and announced, 'Today they are accepting the first-year students into the Octoberists, and Yurii is going to be among them.'

"I was aghast. *His teacher made him do it!* I protested to myself.

"I had been out on the farm cleaning pig pens and was shabbily dressed, but I hurried to the school, afraid I would miss the ceremony, and worried at what might happen to Yurii. My wife and I had warned Yurii's teacher that we would remove him from school if she forced him into the Octoberists against his will.

"I rushed to the school and ran looking everywhere for Yurii, but could not find him. So I went directly to the principal. I reminded him that Yurii did not want to join the Octoberists, and I asked to see my son. The principal retorted, 'I guess you haven't sat in prison long enough, have you?'

" 'If we have to, we will sit in prison for years so our children are not forced to become members of the communist clubs,' I answered.

"From the principal's office, I noticed children down the hall marching into a club room. I looked inside the room and saw that the initiation ceremony was about to begin. I wanted to go inside to be near Yurii, but I knew I did not dare, because I could then be accused of disturbing a public meeting. So I stood outside, looking in and praying.

"Some of Yurii's older classmates saw me and knew I was Yurii's father. At the instruction of their teacher, they stood in front of Yurii to try to shield him from seeing me.

"Painfully I watched as the children marched proudly on stage. The little girls wore freshly starched white aprons. A patriotic song blared from a phonograph turned on full volume. The Young Pioneer members, red scarves tied about their necks, were pinning the red star with an embossed photo of Lenin as a young boy to the shirts of each of the younger children.

"Yurii's turn came. The teacher shoved him out onto

206

the stage. But when one of the Young Pioneers tried to fasten the pin on his shirt, he turned away. The Young Pioneer started to pin the symbol on the other side of his shirt and Yurii shifted again. Finally, Yurii fled from the stage, to the shouts of the teacher and laughter of the students.

"I wanted to comfort my son, but of course I could not see him until he came home that night."

In Barnaul, Christian parents conscientiously attended the parent-teacher association meetings. But frequently school officials turned these meetings into a diatribe against Christianity.

Raisa Y. recalls a PTA meeting where the lecturer raised the stock Soviet slander against Christians. "The *veruiushchie* sacrifice their own children," the lecturer announced dramatically. In gruesome detail, he recounted the story of a ritual murder among believers in Leningrad.

Raisa stood. "Please give me the address in Leningrad where this happened," she asked. "I'd like to go and investigate this myself."

The lecturer reddened. "That is impossible!" he stammered.

"In Barnaul you say that child sacrifices are taking place in Leningrad," Raisa continued before an audience as quiet as night. "In Leningrad, you probably say that we Christians in Barnaul are sacrificing our children. You are acting slyly and dishonestly."

The disconcerted lecturer switched his attack. "Christian children are robbed of their childhood, treated like slaves, and herded to prayer meetings. They are taught psalms instead of merry Pioneer songs. Their backward parents prevent them from attending the theater or participating in the wholesome activities of the Young Pioneers. You Christian parents are spiritually murdering your children. You are maiming their souls!" the lecturer assailed, strangely resorting to religious terminology.

"May I have the names of the Christian students to whom you refer?" Raisa again asked politely. "I would like to check your accusations."

Angrily the lecturer refused.

That afternoon when the PTA meeting finished, the parents and teachers walked by a group of students carrying fireplace logs into the school building. The parents slowed to watch. Four Christian children energetically and enthusiastically led the project.

"Isn't that Sasha R. and Misha N.?" one of the mothers muttered. "Their parents are *veruiushchie,* and look how hard the children work!"

Besides PTA meetings, Christian parents in Barnaul were frequently summoned to school for special conferences. When Lara F. arrived, she was greeted haughtily by her child's teacher. "Your daughter is having difficulty in reading class," she announced. "Your child should receive extra help at home. Do you or your husband know how to read or write?"

Lara said, "Don't assume that because I am a Christian I am ignorant. I have had higher education and am a trained nurse. In fact, we Christians find it hard to believe that intelligent people such as you persist in believing there is no God."

Other parents did not wait for their children's teachers to summon them to school. Every day Irina W.'s ten-year-old daughter Masha came home from school crying. One day Masha's teacher made her stand in a corner until she would promise to wear a red scarf. When Masha refused, the teacher gave her a two (five is the highest mark) on her spelling test, even though Masha had misspelled no words. The day report cards came out, Masha received a three in conduct even though she had not been disobedient. Masha's hardest time came when her teacher campaigned to turn the other children against her. "Masha believes in the devil," the teacher said one day to the students. "Maybe you children should help drive the devil from her!"

In desperation, Irina visited her daughter's classroom. She pled with the teacher not to harass Masha. With tears she turned to the students, "Children, why do you act so cruelly toward Masha and the other Christian children? Have they harmed you in any way? Are they bad students? Are they hindering you?"

Some of the children shouted back, *"Akh*—Masha's nothing but a Baptist!"

By 1972, the situation for Christian school children in Barnaul had continued to worsen. Christian parents wrote:

> How are our children treated in school? Here are some examples: a physics teacher of the 51st school, Zoia Mikhailovna Komarova, in the middle of her lecture, slandered Christian children from Barnaul. After that our children were beaten. Interrogators Rylov, Shtyrev, and others, with the support of the teachers, frightened our children so badly with their questions that they could not even reply.
>
> How could they answer such questions as: "Do you believe in God? Who taught you to believe? Do you pray? Where did you see God? Do you go to church? Where do you gather? Who conducts the services? Who preaches? What does the preacher speak about? Is there a Sunday school? Who teaches the children? How many children attend church?

What are the names of the children? Who conducts the children's services? What kind of program is there for the children?"

If the interrogators are able to pry any information out of the children, it is enough to put a Christian in prison for three to five years. During trials, they try to obtain testimonies from the children against the believers. Besides that, they direct film and television cameras on the children. Later, a long article appears in the newspapers telling how the Christians were exposed at the trial and got what they deserved. After such incidents, some of our children have become sick and some have begun to stutter.

In March, 1972, Vania L. was called to the interrogator's room from his first grade class to be questioned by Investigator Shtyrev. Terrified, the seven-year-old fled and hid in the washroom.

When Vania tried to sneak home quietly, some older children found him and dragged him by the legs up the stairs, his head banging hard on the cement. They triumphantly jerked him into the interrogator's room.

When Vania returned home, sick and shaking, his mother marched to the school. But before she could complain, his flustered teacher said, "Vania did not adequately do his schoolwork today."

"Of course he didn't," Vania's mother countered. "How could he when you dragged him from class to the interrogator's room?"

"I tried to persuade him to finish his work during recess, but he didn't," the teacher protested.

That same day Investigator Shtyrev questioned another boy in front of the child's class and teacher. During the interrogation, the two adults were distracted. When they turned their heads, the Christian boy ran out of the classroom and hid in another room.

A few days later when their frightened children reported that another interrogation was being prepared, a delegation of three Christian parents visited the school. Kirill M., one of the parents, remembers that day.

"When we arrived at the principal's office of the Railroad District school, the communist interrogator Shtyrev was present. He seemed surprised to see us. After we greeted him, we asked directly, 'Who gave you the authority to pressure our children? You are interrogating them about subjects not related to their education. You are violating the Soviet constitution which guarantees separation of the school from the church.'

"Please show us the protocols you have prepared as a result of the interviews with our children," Kirill continued. "We also request to see your documents authorizing you to interrogate our children."

Shtyrev, who was also a KGB officer, shot back, "Who do you think you are that I am going to show you my documents?"

He turned to leave the room, but Kirill spoke again. "If you want to know about the affairs of our church," he continued, "we beg you to ask us adults who are members of the church—not our children."

"We will call any of you for interrogation anytime we please!" Shtyrev raged. "And you can be sure we will continue to question your children. If I don't question them here, I will have them brought by car to my office. We are better equipped for interrogations there," he concluded.

Mariia K., whose six children all attended Barnaul schools, spoke to Shtyrev through tears, "As a mother, I refuse to allow my children to be questioned by you. You have no authorization to interrogate them, ruin their health, and cripple them mentally. My daughter Nadia's health is already destroyed. She has seen you come too many times and take her father away to be questioned by the police. She has watched you ransack our home and tear Christian literature from our hands. Before her eyes, you have threatened to take her and the other children from us. Now, to add to all this grief, you are interrogating her. I will not allow you to do this to my child."

"It doesn't matter what you will allow," Shtyrev ranted. "It is not what you want, it is what we want. If you are not careful, we will invoke Article 19 of the Family and Marriage Law and take your children from you. You are ruining your children by your antisocial behavior."

Kirill spoke quietly, "If that is your decision, comrade, our children are not returning to school from this day on—not until you promise to stop abusing them."

On March 16, 1972, most of the CCECB congregation in Barnaul withdrew their children from school. They immediately sent carefully documented appeals to the Soviet officials in Moscow and to the United Nations explaining their actions. They painstakingly described the suffering of their children. As they had done so often before, they begged that persecution be stopped.

The Christians emphasized their strong desire for their children to return to school, but only "when this disgraceful action ends and a guarantee is given that it will not happen in the future. We parents do not send our children to school to be ridiculed and belittled, but to receive an education."

Not all schoolteachers in Barnaul had supported the interrogations. In fact, some teachers even sympathized with the Christian children but were terrified to oppose the KGB. Nevertheless, all teachers were obligated to teach atheism. In 1971, *Uchitelskaia Gazeta,* the publication of the U.S.S.R. Ministry of Education, had pointed out:

> The 24th Party Congress outlined a clear program of education for a person of a communist society. It is the obligation of every teachers' body to do everything possible to make the atheistic education a constitutent part of a communistic education—to root out with finality superstitions and prejudices among children and to bring up every schoolchild as a militant atheist.[1]

The principal of one school apologized to some Christian parents: "I could do nothing to prevent the interrogation of your children. The KGB simply came and ordered me to give them a room. I heard the interrogator drilling the children as though they were criminals. But there wasn't a thing I could do to stop him, because he represented the government and had authority over me. But believe me—I didn't want to do this to you."

Each day Olga Borisovna,* a teacher who had three Christian children in her class, passed by the place where Galina M., a Christian mother, worked sweeping streets. "I wish you would let your daughter Nadia return to my class," she said with sincerity.

Galina paused from her sweeping and smiled gratefully at the kind teacher. "You know our problem, Olga Borisovna. If the authorities will promise they will not frighten our children in school—that they will not humiliate them and question them like criminals, then we will be happy for the children to return to school. Our children were always at the top of their class. They like

*pseudonym

school and miss their lessons, but we cannot allow the authorities to harm them."

Olga Borisovna was afraid to sympathize openly with Galina. Instead she asked gently, "If I come by your home tomorrow morning and knock on your window, could I just see Nadia for a few minutes? She was my best student. I do miss her. . . ."

That spring Aleksandr Shtertser wrote Soviet authorities on behalf of the congregation to protest against the persecution of Christian schoolchildren in Barnaul. The office of the procurator answered:

> To your letter addressed to the prosecutor of the territory, president of the Altai Territorial Executive Committee, and president of the Presidium of the Supreme Soviet of the U.S.S.R., in which you request an explanation . . . of the interrogation of children of believers by investigatory measures, we declare:
>
> Agencies of the procurator of the territory investigated the criminal case concerning the undertaking of systematic, planned teaching in a Sunday school of children of believers of the Barnaul congregation, a member of the so-called Council of Churches of Evangelical Christians (CCECB).
>
> In the course of the inquiry the investigator questioned children of several believers. The interrogations of children were conducted in conformity with the law, i.e., in the presence of teachers. The physical violence which you mention in your letter was not applied to them.
>
> According to Article 159 of the penal code of the RSFSR, the investigator has the right to question. . . . No exception for children of believers is provided for.
>
> (Signed) B. Krasnoiartsev

The believers understood the procurator's letter. They could expect the Soviet government to show no mercy to their children.

Soon, officials started a campaign to stir public censure against the Christian parents who would not allow their children to return to school. At the believers' places of employment, workers were ordered to discuss the fate of the Christian children.

The authorities spread the accusation that Christians refused to allow their children to attend school because *"religiozniki* are opposed to education." This explanation aroused civic fury, and finally some citizens proposed that Christian children should be taken from their parents by court order.

As a precaution, several Christian parents boarded their children with friends outside the city. However, in April a meeting took place between one of the Christian men and a representative of the County Executive Committee. After this meeting, the believers agreed to bring their children back to their homes.

But they did not send their children back to school. The authorities had offered no assurance that the cruel interrogations and harassments would cease. In fact, the KGB reiterated their threat to remove Christian children from their parents.

This was the final blow. The Christians could withstand persecution themselves, but they would not allow the authorities to endanger the health of their children. They had to take action that would startle the entire world.

On May 9, 1972, twenty Barnaul Baptists stormed the gate of the American embassy in Moscow. The world had to hear their story.

1. "Bringing Up Atheists," *Uchitelskaia Gazeta* (Teacher's Guide), November 13, 1971, p. 1. (Translated in *Religion in Communist Dominated Areas*, Vol. XI, Nos. 7-9, July-August-September, 1972, p. 132.)

EPILOGUE

THE HOURS PASSED SLOWLY as the train pushed back across the endless steppes toward Barnaul. On the trip to Moscow, the Christians had ridden together, strengthening each other with their presence. Viktor's daughter Polina had placed a bright bouquet of violets on the tiny table that unfolded from the wall.

On the return trip, the Christians were divided, and police patrolled their compartments, each of which contained four people. Broadcasts from Radio Moscow blared incessantly over the loudspeakers. The Christians could not leave the sight of their captors for a moment—even to use the washrooms.

During the three-day trip home, police guards were changed three times. Each new group heard the Gospel. The Christians—unsure where they would be taken when the train stopped—prayed, sang, and constantly thanked God for his protection.

Finally the trans-Siberian train halted at Novosibirsk. The Christians climbed off the train and were loaded onto blue buses they hoped would take them home . . . but which they knew could also carry them to a prison camp.

With relief the Christians approached the familiar forest belts and fertile farmlands bordering Barnaul. A crisscross of cheerful parks brightened the austere city ringed with rows of stark cement apartments. A huge star planted in red flowers in front of the railroad station was starting to blossom. The Christians were happy to be home.

But after the bus turned off Vladimir Lenin Prospekt, the city's main street, the driver pulled up in front of a police station. Interrogation resumed.

A KGB officer solicitously took Viktor aside. "How did the Americans treat you? Were they good to your girls? ... Did they give them anything to eat?" he asked, hoping for at least some complaint against the Americans.

It was already night by the time the police finally spat out the words, "Go home! We're finished with you for now."

That night the families who had stayed behind in Barnaul were just returning from a prayer meeting. Yelena saw Viktor and the two girls hurrying down the street toward home. With tears, she embraced her husband, whom she had been prepared never to meet again on earth. She hugged the girls until Polina said her mother was squeezing so tightly it hurt.

The twenty Barnaul believers seemed to have timed their trip to the American embassy well. The eyes of the world were on the U.S.S.R. in anticipation of President Nixon's visit May 22, 1972. Some foreign newspapers carried the believers' plea for help. The BBC and Radio Liberty broadcast their story back into the Soviet Union.

But the news of Nixon's visit overshadowed the pilgrimage of the twenty, and the suffering of Russian

Christians seemed soon forgotten in the West.

The twenty Baptists were not imprisoned for their Moscow visit. But neither were their protests redressed by the Soviet government.

The long-range results of the trip to Moscow may be assessed as follows:

● *Children.* For over a year, Barnaul Christian parents and Soviet authorities struggled. Finally, in the spring of 1973, the church received a letter from the Soviet procuracy stating that the children would no longer be harassed at school. With this guarantee, parents permitted their children to return to school.

But the conflict in Barnaul and across the Soviet Union is far from finished. In July, 1973, Christians wrote from Barnaul, "The future griefs and persecutions awaiting Christians can be imagined by reading the new law on national education. This aims at completely excluding religious influence in the education of children."

In late 1973, a CCECB publication reported that "persecutions of Christian parents are becoming more widespread . . . there have been an increasing number of cases where children are forcibly taken away from their parents and placed in children's homes and boarding schools for atheistic education."

Although few children have actually been removed, this threat still hangs like a dark cloud over every Christian parent in the Soviet Union.

● *Prisoners.* On August 23, 1972, five months after Yurii Mikhalkov was arrested, the evangelist Vladimir Firsov was apprehended. In 1973, local officials also arrested Vladimir Muller from the city of Biisk in the Altai region. He was sentenced for turning in his passport in 1971 and requesting permission to emigrate.

In March, 1974, CCECB leader Georgii Vins was arrested again. Even though gravely ill, he was sentenced the following January to five years in prison and five years in exile.

Yurii Mikhalkov was released from prison in July, 1974, before his term ended—seemingly in response to protest from Christians in the U.S.S.R. and in the West. Both he and former Barnaul presbyter Dmitrii Miniakov, who has now moved to western Russia, remain in poor health. Engineer Mikhalkov is presently employed as a janitor.

To this day, Christians are being arrested in the Soviet Union. In 1976, an estimated ninety CCECB believers served in Soviet prisons. The Council of Prisoners' Relatives continues to plead for their release. In 1974 they wrote:

> At the twilight of the earthly days of the Church of Christ, we come again and again, like Moses, to you Leonid Ilich (Brezhnev) saying: "Let God's people go from the prisons to worship God. Restore what has been taken away, for we do not wish to see you incur misfortunes—the punishment of God which overcame Pharaoh who persecuted those who revered God."

● *Passports.* After the 130 Barnaul Christians turned in their passports, pensioners and mothers with many children no longer received state support. All were prevented from receiving parcels or money orders, using hospitals, changing their residences, buying or selling houses, and in some instances from traveling. They discovered that the authorities would often not allow them to register newborn children. Yelena Rezner and Vladimir Schwarzkopf, who married in 1973, were not permitted to register their marriage because they lacked internal passports.

In some instances, the Christians could not obtain work or continue working. In other cases, fines were levied against them for not possessing their citizenship documents. They survived only through God's provision and the loving support of other churches.

After struggling for almost three years, most of the Barnaul Christians reclaimed their documents in July, 1974, when Yurii Mikhalkov was granted an early release from prison.

● *Emigration.* When all possibility of living as normal citizens in the U.S.S.R. seemed hopeless, some Barnaul Christians of German origin presented a bold appeal to Soviet authorities asking to emigrate—a right technically guaranteed by Soviet laws and international covenants.

In the years following World War II, a trickle of German Russians had been permitted to reunite with relatives in West Germany. From 1957 to 1969 about two thousand six hundred Soviet Germans were permitted to emigrate. After West German Chancellor Willy Brandt's negotiations with the Soviet government, the number increased markedly. In 1972 alone, about three thousand native-born Soviet Germans left Russia. However, this number represented only a small proportion of Soviet Germans wishing to emigrate.

In Barnaul, the Christians knew that only Russians of German origin with relatives in the West held hopes of resettlement in the land of their forefathers. But even with this possibility, not all German-Russian Christians immediately applied to leave. Those who did felt reluctant to leave their brothers and sisters in the Barnaul congregation.

The church as one family prayed and discussed who should apply for permission to emigrate. "Those who could not go did not try to discourage the rest of us. In fact, they stood behind us and tried in every way to help us," explains one of the German Christians who left.

Vladimir K., who was finally permitted to emigrate, hesitated to leave the other believers in Barnaul. "But I realized that for my family—particularly because we are of German descent—there was little hope that my children would ever be able to worship God freely under the Soviet government. For their sakes I felt we must emigrate," he said.

To petition to emigrate, the Barnaul believers sent more than ten letters and telegrams to Kurt Waldheim, general secretary of the United Nations, but never received an answer. On December 12, 1973, they again wrote Waldheim:

> The question of our Christian problem has not been decided, and it is now already the third year that we do not have citizenship papers. For this reason, we request permission to leave the country and emigrate to the Federal Republic of Germany despite the fact that we know we can be dealt with just like Vladimir Muller, who, instead of obtaining permission to emigrate, received an arrest notice and was thrown into jail.
>
> But in these circumstances, too, we cast our hope upon the Lord, who will give us strength in difficult conditions. This present statement would have been signed by many other brothers and sisters. However, knowing the severe reprisals against Christians that we have already experienced ourselves, we believers of German origin have agreed to sign it alone. . . .
>
> Signed by 42 members of the Barnaul church

On December 10, 1974, fifteen members of the Barnaul church again wrote Kurt Waldheim at the United Nations:

> We believers have endured various mockeries and oppressions from authorities. But having turned in our petition to emigrate to West Germany, our circumstances have become worse. We have turned to you many times and also to the Soviet government but haven't received any kind of answer. It is probable that our letters don't pass beyond the borders of our country, since we have on hand only receipts of letters sent but no confirmation that you have received them. In this connection, we are sending you all our written notes with the hope that they will reach you and that you will understand our situation. We ask you to answer our questions and help us in our petitions.

Soviet officials at the Altai Regional Executive Committee demanded that Barnaul believers not write the United Nations about emigrating from the U.S.S.R. "Such questions are settled here," they said. So, the Christians again addressed their petitions to Brezhnev in Moscow:

> If we believers are so hateful to you that you refuse to restore to us our right as citizens and to grant us the freedom of conscience that is guaranteed by the basic law of the constitution of the U.S.S.R., then why don't you do with us as you advise to be done in other countries; that is, give an opportunity to those who would like to leave—and not only to those who have sponsors and an invitation to other countries but to all who would like or desire . . . .
>
> Therefore, we request: (1) that our citizenship problem may be examined according to our demands in previous letters; (2) that a permit be given to the United Nations Commission on Human Rights that they may come to our

country and be convinced of the truthfulness of the facts of persecution of Christians in our country and the need for the restoration of our rights according to the Declaration of Human Rights; and (3) that it be made possible for all those who wish to emigrate to do so.

But like Pharaoh of Egypt, the Soviet authorities continued to stall on their agreement to let German-Russians with relatives in the West emigrate. "It is evident how much we are hated," the Christians complained. "Yet all the activity of the authorities points to the fact that they don't want to give us permission to leave the country.

"Nevertheless, we cannot and will not be silent."

The authorities often insisted that believers could not emigrate without first possessing their documents. In some families, permission to emigrate was granted only to some of the members. In other instances, even when invitations had been received from relatives in Germany, the Soviet government refused to acknowledge these as valid.

When Christians were finally allowed to emigrate, the government did not usually return money, musical instruments, Christian literature, and other confiscated items. Travel arrangements were purposely made as uncomfortable and discouraging as possible, and fees of 400 rubles and higher per person were levied for exit documents.

Igor L. and his family were invited to West Germany by a sister who had been separated from the rest of the family in the Ukraine during World War II. Igor presented his request for emigration with the invitation from his sister to the authorities. "You turned in your passport—you'll never leave," the emigration official sneered.

"God has told me I will leave and so will my family," Igor asserted boldly, although he trembled inside when he saw the official pull a protocol arrest form from his desk. That night Igor dispatched a telegram to the minister of internal affairs in Moscow requesting the minister to intervene with local officials.

Three days later, Igor was summoned to a KGB office. Shaking, he stepped inside. A KGB officer handed him an exit permit, shook hands, and said, "If you can't find an apartment, or they won't give you a job in Germany, please go to the Russian embassy in Bonn and we will be happy to receive you back to Mother Russia."

By 1976 almost all the German-Russians in the Barnaul congregation had emigrated to the West. They consider themselves a voice for the church that continues in Barnaul. A clock hangs in Igor's home in West Germany—a going-away present. The congregation inscribed Proverbs 25: 25 ("As cold waters to a thirsty soul, so is good news from a far country.") to remind Igor's family not to forget the church back in Barnaul.

• *The Way of the Cross in Barnaul.* In June, 1973, Barnaul believers sent a document for U.N. General Secretary Kurt Waldheim to forward to the leaders of the Soviet Union, who had also ratified the International Convention on Civil and Political Rights in 1973.* The letter discusses a meeting which the Barnaul believers had with local authorities in May, 1973, about the disruption of a meeting of pastors in January. In the meeting, a Soviet official named Korobeishchikov denied allega-

*In 1975 the Soviet Union also signed the Helsinki Declaration which includes the following provision: "The participating States will respect human rights and fundamental freedoms, including the freedom of thought, conscience, religion or belief, for all without distinction as to race, sex, language, or religion."

tions by the believers that the police had illegally inflicted violence upon the pastors:

A member of our Barnaul church, Vladimir Firsov, was at this conference. The police had twisted his arms and tried to drag him outside into the freezing cold without outer clothing. Other participants at the conference also suffered violence and were illegally detained at the police station at Liuberetsk.

Three of them, P. D. Peters, A. A. Peterenko, and N. I. Kabysh were arrested and sentenced to three years in prison.

Comrade Korobeishchikov tried to disprove the truth. Crudely distorting the facts, he tried to justify the actions of the police and the authorities, saying our brethren had been treated humanely and had no cause for complaint against the authorities who broke up the meeting. He accused the believers of slander. He asserted that the meeting had not been broken up and that the authorities had acted legally— that force had been used only because the brethren did not immediately hand over all they had with them.

In his speech Comrade Korobeishchikov accused the believers of having contacts with the West and in particular with people working against the Soviet system. . . .

Despite difficulties, the Barnaul CCECB Christians have chosen to remain unregistered, even though an article appeared in *Bratskii Vestnik,* the official AUCECB magazine, in 1973 asserting that "a joyful event in the Barnaul church was the return of the group of believers who were separated from it earlier."

A 1975 issue of *Bratskii Listok,* the CCECB publication, reiterated the reformers' position on registration:

Deciding this question again, we should declare directly and honestly that we are ready to be registered but on the condition of the full separation of church and state and with the observation of principles of our Evangelical Baptist faith which are stipulated in the constitution of the CCECB.

To the present, two congregations are meeting in Barnaul—registered and unregistered. The unregistered congregation now meets at Severozapadnaia Street #144 at the home of former presbyter Dmitrii Miniakov, who presently lives with his family in the Baltic states. Vladimir Lukich Firsov is the current presbyter.

In a recent letter the congregation wrote, "The work of God is continuing. We thank God that at the present, persecutions here have subsided."

However, persecutions against believers continue unabated in some other regions of the USSR. For example, accounts of severe repressions against Christians in Omsk, Siberia, recently have reached the West.

For Russian Christians, struggle and suffering remain a constant possibility—a way of life. In one open letter, Barnaul believers wrote:

> We know that it is written that it is fitting for all who love heavenly truth and desire to live godly in Christ Jesus to suffer. Thus we write this letter, not because we are losing heart (II Corinthians 4:16). On the contrary, in all sorrows we greatly abound in joy and the blessed hope of an early release from all sorrow in the coming of the Son of Man (Luke 21:27, 28). We say to you by the Word of the Lord: "Wherein ye greatly rejoice, though now for a season, if need be, ye are in heaviness through manifold temptations: that the trial of your faith, being much more precious than of gold that perisheth, though it be tried with fire, might be found unto praise and honour and glory at the appearing of Jesus Christ" (I Peter 1:6, 7).

Russian Christians accept the suffering of the cross. However, within the constitution and legal codes of their country, Christians such as the congregation in Barnaul also believe they have an obligation to make their oppression known, even as the Apostle Paul protested centuries before.

In the 13th Bulletin of the Council of Prisoners' Relatives, Russian Christians remind their national leaders:

> We continue to recall and recount all the sufferings of the people of God which result from your instructions. . . . We welcome your concern for the material well-being of the nation, but we condemn your ideological war against believers which has spilled over into an administrative and physical campaign. As far as the heavens are from the earth, so far are your assurances to the world at large about peace, brotherhood, friendship, and freedom from the terrible reality in the U.S.S.R. today.

On January 30, 1974, members of an unregistered church in Slavgorod (central southern Siberia) sent a signed appeal to Kurt Waldheim. Describing brutalities against believers, they wrote, "This is not happening in the Middle Ages, but among us today in the Soviet Union where one of the principles of communism reads, 'Man is to man friend, comrade, and brother.' "

In a fifteen-page appeal to the Presidium of the Supreme Soviet signed in June, 1976, twenty-eight Christians from six different denominations (Pentecostal, Adventist, Baptist, Church of Christ, Roman Catholic, and Russian Orthodox) declared:

> We write this appeal not out of any fear for the future of Christianity. This does not depend on the will of worldly authorities—we have assurances on this count which for us are absolutely certain. The experience of world history shows that all the sufferings that have been inflicted upon

Christianity have served in the last analysis to strengthen and purify it. The experience of our own country in the last half-century also testifies to this.

But it pains us that the present situation of religion in our country is causing serious harm to our nation—and this will become more and more terrible as time goes on. Any sickness is more difficult to cure the longer it is neglected. The abnormality of the situation of religion is the malady of our society.

The aims on which the present attitude of the state to religion is based were developed more than half a century ago, when the total destruction of faith in God was proclaimed as a realistic goal that could be attained in the near future. But life has demonstrated the illusory nature of these hopes. The influence of religion is spreading; young people are being drawn to it. In these new circumstances we must not cling to points of view which life has totally refuted. The attempt to ignore reality is always dangerous, particularly when it concerns one of the central questions in the life of a nation.

We are not the first to make an appeal of this kind, and we are not so naive as to hope that it will be met with instant understanding. But our feeling of responsibility before our country and before history moves us to express our views in the hope that our word will be heard—if not now, then at least before it is too late.

Ivan S., a 70-year-old believer from Barnaul, says, "Persecution of Christians in our country is like waves of the sea . . . it rises and falls . . . and continues to come. But the faithfulness of God is like a mountain—solid and strengthening."

What do Christians in Russia ask of believers in the West? As early as 1971 the Barnaul believers wrote:

229

Dear brothers and sisters, we appeal to you with this letter. We ask you to support us with fasting and prayers in order that your prayers will be incense in the golden bowls (Revelation 5:8) for which the Lord will reward you. We also believe that God will deliver us into his eternal glory in Jesus Christ and will perfect us in temporary suffering. He will confirm, strengthen, and make us steadfast, knowing that God does this for his own sake, wishing to see the faithfulness of his children in order to give us his own glory (Isaiah 48:10-11) and to show that the Lord has true sons. May the man of God be perfect, prepared for every good work (II Timothy 3:17). Grace be with you all. Amen.

GLOSSARY OF RUSSIAN TERMS

All-Union Council of Evangelical Christians-Baptists (AUCECB)—the government-recognized union of about five thousand registered congregations of evangelical Protestants.

babushka—an elderly woman; literally, a grandmother.

Baptist—the popular name for all evangelical Protestants in the Soviet Union; thus, a category equivalent with Orthodox, Catholic, and Muslim.

Council of Churches of Evangelical Christians-Baptists (CCECB)—the unregistered fellowship of evangelical Protestants formed in the 1960s as an alternative to the AUCECB.

druzhinniki—the volunteer auxiliary police.

dvadtsatka—a local church council made up of twenty people.

kolkhoz—a collective, state-owned farm.

Komsomol—the Young Communist League, a social-educational-cultural club for ages 15-28 supervised by the Communist Party.

militsiia—the official police.

Presidium—the 33-member executive committee of the Supreme Soviet. Its chairman is considered Russia's head of state.

Supreme Soviet—the legislative body of the federal government from which the Presidium is selected.

upolnomochennyi—a local representative of the Council for Affairs of Religious Cults.

veruiushchii—a Christian believer.

Znanie—the Society for the Dissemination of Political and Scientific Knowledge, a party-controlled organization for promulgating atheistic teaching.

About the authors

Anita and Peter Deyneka, Jr., are missionaries of the Slavic Gospel Association (Box 1122, Wheaton, IL 60187). Mr. Deyneka is also the executive director of this mission, which sponsors 170 missionaries in 22 countries.

The SGA is responsible for several hundred Christian radio broadcasts transmitted each month into the U.S.S.R. The mission also delivers Bibles and Christian literature into the communist countries and sponsors the only Russian Bible training school in the world.